Pountney

THE BRISTOL POTTERY
AT FISHPONDS 1905–1969

For all the people
who worked at
Pountneys

Pountneys

THE BRISTOL POTTERY AT FISHPONDS 1905–1969

Sarah Levitt

Redcliffe

in association with

City of Bristol Museum & Art Gallery

First published in 1990 by Redcliffe Press Ltd., Bristol in conjunction with City of Bristol Museum & Art Gallery.

Text: Sarah Levitt

Photography: Andy Cotton

Copyright: City of Bristol Museum & Art Gallery

The publishers are grateful for financial help towards the cost of producing this book from:

WAYMAN CERAMICS

The A.M. McGreevy Trust

The Ceramic & Allied
Trades Union

Paul Davis Freight
Services Ltd.

Bainbridge Silencers

ISBN 1 872971 35 0
Typeset and printed by Biddles, Guildford.

Contents

Acknowledgements

Many people and organisations have helped me in the course of this project. I would like to thank them all, especially the following:

Karin Walton, Curator of Applied Art, City of Bristol Museum and Art Gallery, for her guidance and support in all my research and in the preparation of this book.

Kathy Niblett, Senior Assistant Keeper of Ceramics, City Museum and Art Gallery, Stoke-on-Trent, for her comments on my manuscript.

The following, for their help, access to archives and unpublished information, and permission to use copyright material: The *Bristol Evening Post*, Bristol Record Office, John Perks and staff at Cauldon Potteries, Ferrybridge, Yorkshire, The Central Library, Avon County Libraries, The Ceramic and Allied Trades Union, The Design Council, Keele University Library, *Tableware International*.

Harry Frost, Gordon and Irene Hopwood, Gareth Hughes, Robert Pugh and Robert Rankine for information about artists and designers who came to Pountneys.

The following, for kindly lending items illustrated: Mr and Mrs Jarrett, Mrs Keller, Mr Newsom, Mr and Mrs Townsend, Bristol Record Office, Avon County Library Service and three other collectors.

Naomi Beeley, Shaun Cheeseman, Kieran Costello, Nick Dixon, Zoë Edmonds, Louise Evans and Ted Hanscombe for their help in carrying out and transcribing tape-recorded interviews with ex-workers.

Michael Newsom for his generous contribution towards the cost of an exhibition about the Pottery, which was held at Bristol Museum and Art Gallery to mark the publication of this book.

Everyone associated with the Bristol Pottery who took part in this project gave great practical help and tremendous encouragement. I wish I could thank them all, but, sadly, several have died, including Charlie Smith, Ern Dagger and Reg Hanks. I hope that through this book their lifetimes' work will be remembered. The names of all participants, including many who kindly supplied photographs and other material, are listed below.

Mr G.V. Andrews, Miss B.D. Baber, Mrs Lily M. Barton, Mrs Ruby Bodsworth (née Liddington), Mr E.M. Brown, Mrs Carter, Mr Leslie G. Cockram, Mr Alan Coghill-Smith, Mr and Mrs Cyril Coleman, Mr Bernard G. Coombs, Mrs J.E. Cottle, Miss Kathleen L. Cottrell, Mr C. Cox, Miss Phyllis G. Creed, Mr Ted Cumming, Mr and Mrs Ernest Dagger, Mrs Mary E. Davis, Mr Downs, Mrs Eva Duffett, Mr Frederick C. England, Mrs Heather Fletcher, Mrs Hilda M. Ford, Mrs Louvain Ford,

Mr Gilbert French, Mr Ray Gardner, Mrs Gay, Mrs M. Gazzard, Mrs Hazel Gearing, Mr Reg G. and Mr Don Hanks, Mr Charles Harman, Miss Aline Hibbs, Mr Alfred Howe, Ms D.M. Hughes, Mr and Mrs Tom Jarrett, Mr Reg G. Jenkin, Mrs Winifred Joyce (née Mellor), Mrs Hilda McDougall, Mrs Rose McAuliffe, Mrs P.A. Martin, Mr Bernard Moore, Mr Michael J. Newsom, Mrs M. Pearce, Mr L. Powell, Mr Charles J. Pursey, Mr S.F. Roper, Mrs Caroline Scally, Mr Charlie Smith, Mrs Peggy Summerill, Mrs Honor Teague (née Elliot), Mr G. Templar, Mrs Gwen Thompson, Mrs A.M. Tilling, Mrs Cecilie M. Turton, Mr Graham Tyler, Mr Ron Vickery, Mr and Mrs Norman Waters, Mr Ron Watt, Mr Andrew Webster, Mrs M.E. Wheeler, Mrs Frances M. Winslade (née Ashman), Mr George Wood, Mr Raymond Wood, Mrs Young.

Only time prevented us from interviewing more people. Any other ex-workers who wish to do so are encouraged to send written memories of Pountneys to Bristol Museum and Art Gallery, where they will be added to its collection of documentary material about the Pottery. The Central Library, College Green and Bristol Record Office also have material relating to the Pottery.

Introduction

The Bristol Pottery, Pountneys' model factory, was built at Fishponds in 1905 and closed in autumn 1969. The closure brought an end to a continuous tradition of potting in Bristol which went back for well over 300 years. This is the story of the Fishponds factory, designed on revolutionary new principles by T.B. Johnston to replace his out-dated premises on Saint Philip's Marsh. Through his efforts this venerable old firm was revitalised, becoming once more a prosperous and important concern.

The story is told through documents gathered from a variety of sources, since most of the firm's own archives were lost during, and in the years following, its closure. Examples of its products still survive in many homes and the City of Bristol Museum and Art Gallery has built up a small collection of pottery which helps to tell the tale. Life is breathed into the bare bones of history, however, by the ex-workers themselves, 60 of whom were interviewed in preparation for this book. They not only gave their time, memories and encouragement, but also lent many of the photographs which, more than anything else, help to recapture the feeling of life at Fishponds. This book is their story and it would not have been possible without their help.

Note on illustrations and footnotes

All 'X' numbers refer to the City of Bristol Museum and Art Gallery's collection of photographic negatives. All 'N' and 'G' numbers refer to its applied art collection, whilst all objects without numbers are from private collections. Please refer to acknowledgements for details of lenders. Bristol Record Office is referred to as BRO and Bristol Museum and Art Gallery as BMAG. Firm dates are given where items bear an impressed datestamp.

The Victoria Pottery and before

The name Pountney had only been associated with the Bristol Pottery since the early 19th century, but the firm took great pride in being the oldest pottery manufacturer in the country. In 1914 excavations at the site of a 17th century pottery at Brislington, just outside Bristol, revealed a tin-glazed earthenware fragment bearing the date 1652.[1] In 1683 one of the Brislington potters, Edward Ward, set up the Temple Back Pottery at Water Lane on Temple Back in Bristol. This passed through a succession of owners until John Decimus Pountney went into partnership with Henry Carter in 1813.

The Temple Back Pottery was one of several enterprises in Bristol producing tin-glazed earthenware. In 1786 its new owner, Joseph Ring, began making creamware, a considerably more refined product developed in Staffordshire and popularised by Josiah Wedgwood. This enabled the Pottery to flourish and keep up with the demands of an increasingly sophisticated market-place.

Under John Decimus Pountney the firm, now known as the Bristol Pottery, entered a period of great prosperity. As well as being a remarkable industrialist he was a councillor and alderman, serving as Mayor in 1847. In 1852 he collapsed after supervising the firing of a kiln and died a few hours later in his manager's house. His widow, Charlotte, devoted herself to the firm for the next 20 years. Their son, the ceramic historian W.J. Pountney, wrote of her:

> . . .she was constantly defrauded of considerable sums of money, and in the end one of the clerks, who was quite young, disappeared with a sum of money amounting to nearly £1,400. My mother made no attempt to prosecute him, as his widowed mother, who was a very old customer at the pottery, would have suffered more than the son. She bore her losses bravely for a little time, but as she was in failing health, and much depressed owing to the competition in business, she was at length induced by her solicitor to sell.[2]

The Bristol Pottery was sold in 1872 and Mrs Pountney died the following year. It was sold again six years later to Patrick Johnston and a Mr Rogers, two London solicitors. Instead of halting the firm's decline, they presided over its bankruptcy.

Enter T.B. Johnston

Thomas Bertram Johnston, a nephew of Patrick Johnston, had also been intended for a legal career, but in 1882 family circumstances forced him to accept a job at his uncle's Pottery. The retirement of Mr Rogers in 1883 and the death of Mr Johnston in 1884 left the young man at the helm of:

> . . .an old firm with great traditions, but inconvenient and out-of-date works, and immediate prospects such that only a man of exceptional force and ability in the optimism of early youth could have faced them.[3]

Johnston, affectionately known as 'TB', was a remarkable character. Remembered as a 'great big built bloke' who weighed 25 stone in later life,[4] his ideas were as grand as his stature and he was never hesitant in expressing them. Johnston had a scientific mind and a passion for order. However, 'Always a man to grasp the importance of new ideas, he was cautious in their application'.[5] He was described as clear-sighted and hard-working, with immense knowledge and vitality. Even as a bedridden old man, it was he who ordered the first continuously fired tunnel ovens, only months before his death in 1938. As if one pottery was not enough, early in his career he bought the Bovey Tracey Pottery in Devon, which operated as a sister company until its closure in 1957.

Johnston's energy overflowed into politics. He was one of the first supporters of Joseph Chamberlain's campaign for the re-introduction of import tariffs and sold pottery decorated with humorous caricatures on the subject. Johnston even stood for Parliament on one occasion, but as his obituary in *The Times* commented:

> It was the economic problems of politics that alone attracted him. Among the more prominent objects of his hearty prejudices were bankers, economists, Liberal politicians, free trade, and the gold standard. . .
>
> His prejudices and the force with which he expressed them did not make enemies. He once attacked in the Press with characteristic candour an eminent banker. . . The banker replied, first, with the threat of libel action; next, with the suggestion of an interview; and finally with an invitation to join the board of the bank.[6]

Johnston's employees were equally charmed:

> He would fraternise with the men, you see, talk to people. He was very well respected. When he came the word would go from the front of the factory right down to the bottom that he was about.[7]
>
> He was a fine man. . . If a workman had any complaints he could go and talk to the boss. He didn't always get satisfaction!. . . He looked for quality. He'd admire your work. When I was a young fellow he'd come round and say 'Very good indeed'.[8]

Johnston 'could always see the other fellow's point of view'.[9] Deeply interested in industrial relations, in 1917 he was a key figure in the formation of the Joint Industrial Council by the pottery manufacturers and trade union. In 1920 the Bristol Pottery was one of the first to set up a Works Committee, following the recommendations of the Whitley Report, and he encouraged membership of trades unions. His vision of an ideal factory encompassed not only all the latest production methods, but also welfare facilities. A canteen, sports ground and a social club were eventually provided, but his dream of building 50 or 60 workers' houses, 'Bournville'-style, was never realised.[10]

Soon after inheriting his uncle's business, Johnston decided to sell the 200-year-old Temple Back Pottery and move to temporary premises while looking for a suitable site on which to build a completely new factory, and a financial backer to pay for it. The Victoria Pottery, built in 1865 on Saint Philip's Marsh, behind Temple Meads station, was on the market and the Bristol Pottery moved there in 1886. By then, Johnston had paid off his debts and the firm began to prosper again. Catalogues show a flourishing business in domestic earthenware.[11]

In 1889 Pountney & Co. Ltd. was formed with Johnston and Charles Burns as joint managing directors. Burns had been taken on as a clerk around 1864. His contribution must not be forgotten. W.J. Pountney ascribed his success to 'his industry, his close attention to business and his other valuable qualities'.[12] One of these was probably thrift, since he was remembered as a 'skinflint'.[13] Burns, who died in 1911 or 1912, remained at Johnston's side for 30 years.

The proprietor of the Victoria Pottery never lost sight of his ambition to build an up-to-date works elsewhere, and over the years he gradually formulated his plans. He revised and revised the designs, which he used to carry around in his pocket ready to show anyone who expressed the slightest interest. Johnston's own resources were insufficient for the project and all attempts to obtain financial backing failed.

> The money, however, which Mr Johnston was not able to obtain on ordinary business lines, came to him through an extraordinary piece of good luck. A friend of his, Mr Heward Bell, who had come into a large fortune, told him that he found the possession of so much money a great responsibility, and he would like to do something which would be of real benefit to the community; that he had turned over many things in his mind, but what appealed to him most was the model pottery, which he, Mr Johnston, had so long talked about.[14]

W.H. Bell, whose friendship with Johnston stemmed from their mutual interest in cricket, joined the Board of Directors in 1900. Soon afterwards an eight-acre site was acquired in Fishponds, six miles north-east of Bristol, and preparations to build the new factory began in earnest.

NOTES

1. Fragments dated 1647 and 1649 have since been found, but Pountneys never referred to these dates in their publicity.
2. W.J. Pountney, *Old Bristol Potteries*, 1920, p. 132. Facsimile edition by E.P. Publishing Ltd., 1972.
3. *The Times*, obituary, 18.2.38.
4. Hanks.
5. Company type-sheet by Harold Counsell, 1959, p. 10.
6. Loc. cit.
7. England.
8. Smith.
9. Counsell, loc. cit.
10. *Pottery Gazette*, October 1920, p. 1351.
11. BRO 20165/13–19.
12. Pountney, op. cit. p. 134.
13. Hanks.
14. *Pottery and Glass*, July 1945, offprint.

A tour around a 'model' factory

Fishponds had been a coal-mining village, but by 1905 the mines were exhausted and land around the pit heads was being sold for other industrial purposes. Pountneys' site on Lodge Causeway lay near to main roads, the railway and the coal mines of Kingswood. Bristol was rapidly expanding; its tramlines now reached Fishponds and the miles of terraces being built there would provide a ready supply of labour. Around 700 people were employed at the factory in its heyday, about half of whom were women. The site had some drawbacks. There was no water supply and so at first rainwater was collected from the roofs. It also stood at the top of a long hill. Extra trace horses were kept at the bottom to help pull the carts which toiled up the road all day bringing coal, flints or clay from Fishponds station. The horses, with their straw hats, were much loved but a pitiful sight; in summer they occasionally dropped in their shafts from exhaustion.

Visitors to the factory would first enter the lodge, which housed the lodge-keeper, the board room and a small museum of ceramics. There T.B. Johnston would hold court with his fellow directors. These included his son Patrick, who joined the firm in 1925 and was responsible for design and sales. Another young man, Johnston's nephew Alick Newsom, started in 1919 and by the 1930s was supervising the production side.

Groups touring the works passed the showrooms and offices before reaching the factory floors, where they could follow all the stages of manufacture. Most processes remained basically the same over the factory's 60-year existence.

Single-storey buildings with raked roofs and skylights, such a feature of the 20th century urban landscape, were still an exciting new concept; any industry could be divided into a series of processes which turned raw material fed in at one end into a finished article which came out at the other. A journalist commented that the new premises 'would do for any one of a dozen manufacturing industries.'[1]

The factory made a striking contrast with the rambling old 'pot-banks' of Stoke-on-Trent, the centre of the ceramics industry. Some forward-looking firms were making improvements, but many potteries had cramped workshops huddled around the kilns, accessible only by winding exterior staircases. Industrial diseases were rife in such places. The new building provided a healthier environment, with light, well-ventilated work-rooms.

Pountneys, far from the industry's main centre, was known in the trade as an 'out-potter'. As such they found it more economical to process their own raw materials than to rely on the specialist suppliers of Stoke-on-Trent. They made all their own glazes, a process involving spectacular displays of pyrotechnics. China stone and granite were ground in huge mills, then added to different clays and flint in varying quantities according to the required mixture, or 'body'. The clay, in dust, solid or liquid 'slip' form, was then sent to the various departments.

Production processes

One of the unique features of T.B. Johnston's factory was that interior tiles, lavatories and wash-basins were made alongside tableware and toughened pottery for institutional use. Although they had different firing requirements, they all went through the same kilns.

Tile-making

Glazed white tiles were made until World War II. Cyril Coleman, who started as a wheel-turner on a tile machine at the age of 14 in 1926, remembered the process. His job was to stand on a platform and turn a huge wheel, which brought down 20 tons of pressure onto a metal mould or 'die', containing powdered clay. The tiles were white, with no decoration.

Sanitary casting

Sanitary casting was an extremely heavy trade and so only men worked in the department until the 1940s, when a few women were employed making small hand-basins. The 'slip-casting' method was used from the 1920s onwards. Plaster moulds, held together with metal strips, were filled with a liquid 'slip' from hoses. The clay was left to settle as water was absorbed by the mould. Excess slip was poured away and the clay shape allowed to dry slightly before the mould was removed. After further drying, the rough edges were sand-papered. Each man had a variety of moulds for sinks and lavatory-pans. He would be expected to make 11 casts a day; out of a week's work it was usual to damage five or six pieces.

'Making'

Most workers made domestic crockery. It took around three months for a piece of clay to pass through all the processes, during which time it might be handled by 36 people. Pountneys made dinner- and tea-services, ewers and bowls, slop-pails and chamber-pots, and some ornaments. The 'making-shops' turned out three types of pottery: flat-ware, such as plates, hollow-ware, such as cups, and complicated shapes like sauce-boats. In the early days these would be press-moulded with solid clay, in the same way that a child makes an impression with 'Plasticine'. Slip-casting, introduced in the Edwardian era, eventually superseded this technique. Another old trade, that of the lathe-turner, who shaped the foot-rims of better quality vessels, also disappeared with the advent of slip-casting.

The plate-maker had three assistants. The 'batter-out' made the 'bat' of clay which was put on a convex plaster-of-Paris mould. The 'maker' put this on a rotating machine called a 'jigger' and brought down a profile tool which shaped the back of the article. The 'mould-runner' marked the date on the finished plate then took it, still on the mould, to dry in a stove:

> You'd put two on the shelf and take two out that had been dried, you'd go back with the moulds, take the plates out and stack them by the side and he used the moulds again. . . I'm talking about hundreds of plates a day, mind, not a few, hundreds![2]

The 'fettler' then smoothed the rough edges. This created a lot of dust, but fettlers at Bristol worked under hoods with extractor fans. Cups were made on a 'jolley' by a similar process, but the mould formed the outside of the vessel and the profiling tool was brought down inside to create the interior shape. Each maker paid his own team. Graham Tyler, remembering the 1920s, commented:

> Of course there was only one earning the money to pay the batter-out, the mould-runner and the fettler out of their wages. You had to keep at it to keep your people earning. Your wages depended on the quality of your assistants. . . At one time I had three women and a boy. Well, I'd always keep that boy sweet; I always gave him two-and-sixpence in the middle of the week. That he would look forward to, it was a good part of his wages. He'd keep good time and do a good day's work with a little bit of encouragement.

Mould-runners, generally boys and girls aged 13–15, had one of the worst jobs, running backwards and forwards all day. School-leavers tended to spend a year or so mould-running before being apprenticed to a specific trade. Rose McAuliffe, who started in 1907 at 14, soon found herself in charge of her own gang:

> Well, my sister worked there, making saucers, and she wanted an attendant, and of course me knowing that it was my sister, of course off I went. . . After a bit the foreman said 'I'm going to put you on the bench'. I said, 'I don't want to go!'. I cried; I didn't want the responsibility. He said to my sister, 'Ada, I'm doing her a good turn but she don't know it!'

In the 'handling' department men made large handles from clay squeezed through a machine into strips, cut to length and deftly bent into shape. Teacup handles would be made in a mould and applied by females, who were considered more suited to this delicate work. Skill was needed to position the handle exactly with the right consistency of slip; Ray Wood commented, 'I used to stick a handle on and I could pick the jug up by the handle and it wouldn't fall off.' He also formed the lips on jugs, which needed careful shaping to pour well and resist chipping:

> They used a lot down Weston-super-Mare, hotels and places like that, and the actual lip used to get a knock...When they pointed it out I said, 'That's easy, all you've got to do is run your thumb round the edge of it and take a bit off and you won't get it'. They didn't have the problem afterwards.

New methods speeded up production, but such individual touches were no longer possible. Mr Tyler described how the art of turning died following the introduction of slip-casting:

> The complicated things which we used to do on the lathe, I turned the original and handed that original over to the mould-maker. He would block it, then it was cast, sponged and fettled by women and didn't come back to the lathe. That was a revolution, improving the processes, and economically it was much cheaper. There were three of us on the turning section and eventually it came to the point when there wasn't sufficient work to keep us going. They wanted more soup-dishes for government orders at that time and so I moved over to that section.

Firing

Wet, unfired pottery is called 'green' and so the finished ware would be carried on boards on the potters' shoulders to the 'greenhouse', where it was allowed to dry before firing. Most pottery is fired several times. The first, or 'biscuit', firing fixes the clay into a permanent shape. This takes two or three days and a temperature of 1250°C is reached. The second, or 'glost', firing sets the glassy coating or glaze, which makes the ware impervious to moisture. Sometimes pottery is only decorated before glazing, but if decoration is applied on top of the glaze then a third firing is needed, in a lower-temperature 'enamel' kiln, to fix the colours.

The men who loaded and unloaded the huge bottle ovens were called 'placers'. The aristocrats of the pottery workforce, they had to be strong and well-built to cope with the unremitting toil of their work. The ware would be loaded into 'saggars', coarse fireclay containers. It took two days for a gang to load an oven with around 2000 of them. A full saggar, which could weigh half a hundredweight, had to be picked up and carried on the head through a small door into the kiln. A placer then climbed a ladder to put the saggar on top of a pile of up to 20 others. The saggar was supported on an old hat and a 'doughnut' of wadding. Charles ('Paddy') Harman remembered getting ready for his first day in 1944:

16

They told me I'd be starting and what it involved, so I went down to Old Market and bought an old trilby hat. You had to turn the sides up and then you got a thick elastic band which you wrapped an old stocking round until you had a pad sufficiently thick to keep the weight of your saggar off your head. The first time I didn't have sufficient stockings on; I clonked it on my head and of course I nearly knocked myself out!

We had to go up huge ladders, but I couldn't do it! Ernie Dagger was the foreman. 'Go on Paddy, take a chance!' he said. I'd go up and I'd get so far and I'd start to panic a bit; I was clutching onto the steps for dear life you see! Gradually you learnt how to carry by just adjusting your neck. You moved your neck around and you didn't use any hands at all. At first you kept on going, holding the saggar with one hand, and then it happened one day you'd go up the ladder and somebody would say something and you'd turn round...then you'd suddenly think 'Oh! I've taken my hand away!' From then on it was quite simple.

Ernest Dagger was an affectionately remembered figure. His family had been potters for generations and he worked on the biscuit ovens for 46 years, 20 of them as foreman, or 'cod-placer'. Another well-known character was an old man called Joe Whitely who had the important task of firing the ovens. The fireman would stay nearby, day and night, stoking the coal; ten tons were needed to fire one ton of pottery. He would also test the temperature by taking out clay rings with an iron rod poked through a hole; success or failure, which involved hundreds of pounds' worth of ware, depended on his judgement. Joe Whitely was as 'skinny as a rake' and the sweat which poured off him as he worked through the night would be replenished from 'flagons of cider which he'd dilute and dilute – stick them under a dirty old tap'.[3] The heat would blast through the tiny trial hole left in the kiln door after it had been bricked up for the firing. No-one else could bear to look down it, but the fireman would put in his rod and draw it out red hot with a trial ring on the end and his hands frizzling.

The oven was left to cool and then emptied. In normal circumstances this was an unpleasantly hot task, but when speed was needed the men would be paid 'hot money' for working in a temperature of 125°F or more. They stripped to the waist, mufflers round their necks to mop up the sweat. Biscuit ware was bedded in the saggars with fine sand and this ran down their backs, eating into the skin. They bound their hands with rags but after a few hours they would be raw and bleeding.

The development of tunnel kilns transformed the work of placers. The ware, loaded on trolleys, was fired as it moved slowly through a long tunnel. This was a continuous, dependable process and so the rush to fill and empty the bottle ovens and the risks involved in their firing became things of the past. Only one other tunnel kiln was said to be in use in this country when Pountneys built their first in 1938. Used for glost-firing, it was 220 feet long and powered by gas from their own production plant. An electric enamel tunnel kiln was installed later that year.

The biscuit warehouse
A team of women sorted the ware as they emptied the saggars and it was put in the biscuit warehouse. Pottery was made more or less continuously, but only decorated in response to orders. The women dusted off the sand, and separated 'easy-fired' ware, which had been at the bottom of the oven, from 'hard-fired', taken from the top. Easy-fired ware was decorated before glazing since it absorbed pigments more easily, whilst hard-fired ware was glazed before being decorated.

Underglaze decorating
Underglaze decoration is protected by the glassy surface and so it cannot be worn away in use, but because it has to withstand the high-temperature glost firing, a limited range of colours used to be available. Overglaze decoration is less durable, but the colours can be brighter and more varied and overglaze-printing processes are capable of greater subtlety. All gilding is done over the glaze.

Printing
Copper-plate printing on ceramics involves three skills; engraving the patterns with punches and fine chisel-like tools onto plates or rollers, printing them on tissue paper and transferring them from the paper to the ware. Engravings were usually bought ready-made, but Pountneys employed their own engravers because they specialised in 'badge-ware', with crests and other motifs specially printed for customers.

Reginald Hanks, for many years head-engraver, began his apprentice-ship in 1909. Reg Hanks designed all the different badges and numerous tableware patterns. Creating a completely new line was a daunting task. Every piece needed its own specially shaped borders and centres and it might take a week to produce the design for one plate.

From the 1950s Reg Hanks was the only engraver at Bristol, and indeed one of a diminishing band in the pottery industry as a whole. There is still a demand for traditional engraving, but photography, lithography and silk-screening are more generally used today.

Bert Thorne, in charge of underglaze printing until well past retirement age, was 'a very able man who knew the state of wear of all his rollers and how strong to mix the colour so the eventual colour-matching of the various pieces was satisfactory'.[4] Steps led up to Mr Thorne's office, where the printing was done on a roll of tissue paper. This went down through a slit in the floor and was cut into lengths as it emerged. The prints, which had to be used while still tacky, were hung on lines so that they did not stick together.

Hazel Gearing, a transferer, commented that the office was 'kept private up there because, naturally, he was a craftsman, he was on his own'. This was a common practice in potteries, but a photograph of the Victoria Pottery[5] shows that the printer at one time worked alongside the female transferers. By the 1930s they did not have a formal apprenticeship, although it took about six months to learn the trade. Each transferer had an assistant who 'cut out the patterns and did all the hard work. The actual transferer put them on; that was a trade'.[6] She gently rubbed them down with soft soap and a felt pad. Her skill lay in knowing where all the parts went for hundreds of different patterns and items and imperceptibly joining the continuous borders; 'If your join wasn't straight they wouldn't touch it up and let it go, it was thrown out and smashed!'. Her assistant then vigorously rubbed the tissue with a hard brush to transfer the pattern. Each piece was washed to remove the paper and put in a small kiln to burn off the oil in the colours.

Underglaze painting

With underglaze painting the colour soaks into the biscuit clay like ink on blotting paper. The slightest brush mark becomes indelible and stylised freehand patterns in fast, economical strokes are the most effective. These were very much in vogue at the start of this century, and so the technique, which had fallen into disuse, was revived. Encouraged by Cecil Garland, assistant decorating manager from 1933, and J.F. Price, a freelance design consultant, a style evolved loosely based on the old tin-glazed earthenware patterns. This continued to be a Bristol speciality until the 1960s.

Schoolgirls with an aptitude for art were taken on in batches of five or six. They were apprenticed for four years, until 1929, when the training period was shortened. In the 1930s Seraphima Hamblin, a Russian *émigrée*, led a small team of highly skilled paintresses including Frances Ashman and Mary Breacher. Female labour was cheap, but one or two men, referred to as 'the artists', were also employed, such as Charlie Smith, a well-known character at Pountneys for over half a century.

The patterns were painted with soft, long brushes that made broad sweeping strokes or fine lines depending on the pressure applied. The colours were ground with a palette knife and mixed with water and gum. Complicated designs were laid out by dusting charcoal through perforated paper patterns called 'pounces'. Each paintress had her own characteristic style and always painted complete sets so that they matched. Some women worked in the 'band-and-line' shop, painting continuous broad and narrow stripes with the aid of a turntable. The rough biscuit ware made their fingers sore and 'they used to put sticky paper on their fingers that would go round the edge of the plate to do the bands'.[7]

Some patterns were more lucrative than others. 'You were lucky if you got a good pattern. The forewoman would look through the book to see what order was needed and it was chance what you got.'[8] Identification numbers were painted below the four-figure pattern number on the back of each piece and the paintresses' pay would be calculated when their work reached the glost warehouse. A close eye was kept on quality. Underglaze paintresses were particularly at the mercy of the glaze dippers:

> One dipper liked to get people into trouble to get in with the bosses. He knew if you waggled the plates and cups around in a certain way the colours would run. If the ware was extra hard-fired he knew very well that those cups would run... We got the blame for it, for not putting enough gum in our colour. If we put too much gum in we couldn't work the colour at all.[9]

When accidents happened a whole day's pay could be lost:

> I was teaching one girl one time; she was watching me doing teapots and it was a really difficult pattern. She said could she watch me. I just finished this line of teapots and somehow or other her hand went in and smashed three or four... I counted to ten before I spoke to her! She was a dear little girl really. I was ever so annoyed. I'd put all my heart and soul into that pattern and it was a badge pattern that would have to be printed again and brought back to me.[10]

Glazing

Bert Duffett, foreman dipper and 50 years with the company, had about ten people under him, dipping the ware by hand in vats of glaze. 'For plates and saucers we used to have a hook tied on our thumb to hold them',[11] as they were dipped and skilfully twisted to create a smooth surface of exactly the right thickness. Most tableware was glazed in white, ivory or cream. Lead poisoning was a serious hazard for dippers until the present century when government regulations controlled the use of lead in glazes. Pountneys developed a lead-free glaze in 1905, but lead was still used for some purposes. Women were first employed alongside male dippers in the early 1920s. Eva Duffett, one of the first, remembered: 'Before I started it used to take seven years' apprenticeship, but when they took on girls you didn't work an apprenticeship, you just learnt naturally.'

Glost firing

Another group of skilled workers, the 'crankers', set the glazed pottery in saggars ready for glost firing. This had to be done in such a way that the pieces did not touch and fuse together in the heat. Small fireclay devices called 'stilts' and 'thimbles' were used to keep them apart.

The glost-placers' work was even heavier than that of the biscuit placers, since the ware was now covered with glaze. Discolouration from smoke and specks of soot was a problem with the old coal-fired kilns and so, to keep the air out, 'wads' of clay were sandwiched between the saggars as they were piled up.

The glost warehouse

Some items were finished after glost firing, but others would be sent to the overglaze-decorating department and then to the enamel kiln before arriving at the finished-stock warehouse.

Warehouse work was hard; great piles of plates were carried to and fro and there was much running up and down ladders. The initial sorting involved knocking sharp points of glaze from the backs of plates where the 'thimbles' had touched them:

> The girls sat on upturned boxes in circles, a piece of cloth covering one's lap, a dozen or so plates upside down, an iron flat tool for chipping bits off, a stone to smooth it. Some pieces were sandy, crazed, cracked or 'whirlers', these were rejected. The rest were piled on trolleys and stacked in the warehouse. . . This was full of containers called bins, very large, about three high, back to back, about six each side of a central gangway. Each shape had a name and each pattern painted or transferred on it had a number. The girls selected sets to be decorated, those for hand-painting or 'best gold' being chosen carefully.[12]

Some faults could be repaired by polishing on a wheel or re-glazing. Rejects which could not be sold as 'seconds' were destroyed:

> Baskets and baskets of ware were smashed. We'd smash it up small, take it all out to the weighing machine. They used to use it on the roads, up in Fishponds. Some of the stuff that looked good we thought 'We won't smash that', we'd put it out on the wall for different people to take that was really hard up.[13]

Seconds might be purchased by employees, who were entitled to 'cash-sales' every so often; otherwise they were sold locally. The main outlet for Pountneys' seconds, known as 'lump', was Fletchers of Stapleton Road.

Glost-warehouse girls were in a good position to buy things, but there was eager competition. Mrs Gazzard remembered:

21

They did a lovely pattern once of all forget-me-nots – salt and pepper and dinner stuff. I thought, 'I'll have that salt and pepper for our dinner' – you know the little group of us at work – and we had a salesman come in from another place, and he went and bought the salt and pepper for himself!

The chance to meet sales representatives and retailers gave additional interest to the lives of the girls in the office and finished-stock warehouse. Pountneys' five sales representatives who toured the country might not return with full order-books, but some always brought back a fresh repertoire of spicy stories!

Overglaze decorating

Most overglaze painting was done by a team of girls. In the 1930s Doris Wathen was in charge. They coloured prints, applied stamped patterns and added the finishing touch of a fine line in gold or a colour round rims and handles. All the gilding was done here, in ordinary or 'best' qualities. 'Best', which contained real gold, had to be burnished with silver sand after firing. Again, a few male 'artists' worked separately, producing high-quality freehand designs. Some of the finest painting was done by Albert Pollard, another long-serving employee. He also 'aerographed' patterns, with large blocks of sprayed colour or subtle shading. Gwen Thompson remembered how 'he would get a little bit of cotton wool and wisp it around to make lovely clouds. He could create wonderful things, really works of art.'

The paintresses' work called for artistic flair, a steady hand and a great deal of patience. It took months to reach the required proficiency:

We used to practise with what they called Persian red paint. We had to grind it up on a tile with turps until it was smooth. Then we used to have a wheel [to stand the ware on] and we used to practise lines all day long for weeks on end. Then they'd let us do a couple of pieces to see what it turned out like. Then we'd practise strokes down the handles and then they'd let us do small orders until we'd start the real jobs.[14]

Gwen Thompson remembered her first day in 1930:

My friend Kathleen arrived with her cookery apron on that she had from school, but I didn't arrive with anything at all. They said, 'Well, you'll have to get an overall.' In those days the shops stayed open very late and I suppose it was six o'clock before I got home. But there was time to buy one. I was very pleased with it – a nice bright pink with checked collar and cuffs. But it soon got dabs of paint over it; it didn't stay pristine for long!

Mrs Cottle remembered that 'some had flowers and some had plain.' Her mother used to 'despair trying to get the paint out.' The girls also bought their own palette knives and paintbrushes, traditionally called 'pencils':

> Mr Garland used to keep the brushes in the office and we had to get a little brush, a 'tracer' they called it, and they were either tuppence or threepence each. Then you had to have a 'liner' to put a line on with, that was shaped diagonal – they were fourpence each. Then there was a 'shader' which you used when you were more experienced. You had to put it on in a way that one side of a flower would be deep pink then it would fade to very pale.[15]

Rags were brought from home to rub out mistakes. This could be done on a glazed surface, whereas with biscuit ware all marks were indelible. Some paintresses hated the rough feel of unglazed pottery and would not have worked in the underglaze department. There were other differences; underglaze colours were water-based, but overglaze ones were mixed with aromatic oils which, together with turps and fat-oil, created a distinctive aroma: 'As you went through the office where you clocked on you could begin to smell the gold, a peculiar smell it was, and the turps. It smelt like home!'[16]

Liquid gold was held in a little glass 'shell'. Every trace would be carefully wiped up with rags which would then be sold for metal reclamation. Its cost was continually impressed on the trainees, but one girl got into deep trouble when she inadvertently picked up the gold brush during an illicit game of noughts and crosses![17]

Printing

Printing was also carried out in this department, either with traditional tissue-paper transfers or multicoloured 'lithographic' transfers which came ready-printed. In the 1930s the overglaze printer was Mr Linton, who worked at the end of the room with his assistants, and the transferers worked along one side, separated from the paintresses by the 'stillages', or racks holding boards of finished ware. Sometimes overglaze printing would be hand-coloured, but 'lithos' were used in increasing quantities. Lithography, a method of printing with stone blocks, was first used for decorating pottery in the 1880s. Transfers came on a paper backing sheet. This was soaked off with a sponge and the patterns were carefully placed face-upwards on the ware, which had already been prepared with a sticky size. Many firms bought transfers from Germany, but Pountneys were among the few to design and make their own. They benefited from this during the First World War, when German transfers were unavailable. At one time they even exported lithographic transfers to America. However, by the late 1930s the trade was becoming highly specialised and Pountneys ceased production.

The 'litho' and overglaze-painting sections worked closely together. The litho girls used to save their backing sheets for the paintresses to pin onto their work-benches on Saturday mornings during their general clean-up in preparation for the following week. Trainee paintresses were often sent to collect the heavy rolls of transfers from a works on Saint Philip's Marsh where they were made. Gwen Thompson and her friends:

> . . .would have a bit of fun on the way, then we would have to decide whether to go on the bus; the firm would pay our bus fare, or go by rail to Saint Philip's station. It was all right, but coming back with those heavy rolls wasn't quite so funny!

Packing

The factory was full of mice, which came from the railway cuttings nearby. Mrs Gazzard once took the lid off a teapot and 'out popped a little mouse!'. They used to nest in the straw in the packing department, where they were killed by the resident cats. These caused further problems, however, when they had kittens in the straw.

In the pre-cardboard box era crate-making was an important trade. Stacks of hazel withies used for the crates were much in evidence around the building. The wood had to be soaked in a pond then bent and held together with wire. The crockery was packed in damp straw, sometimes accompanied by notes from the warehouse girls! The crates, which were returnable, would be opened on the pavements outside china shops, and passers-by had to step around all the crockery and straw. As a 1957 publicity leaflet noted: 'The Bristol Pottery is justly proud of its unrivalled reputation for packing. Crates often go to the other end of the world without a single piece being broken in transit.'[18]

NOTES

1. *Pottery Gazette*, September 1905, p. 1006.
2. England.
3. Harman.
4. Newsom.
5. BMAG X10, 152A.
6. Gearing.
7. Smith.
8. Anon.
9. Anon.
10. Creed.
11. Duffett.
12. Hughes.
13. Gazzard.
14. Cottle.
15. Ibid.
16. Thompson
17. Ibid.
18. Private collection. Copy in BMAG.

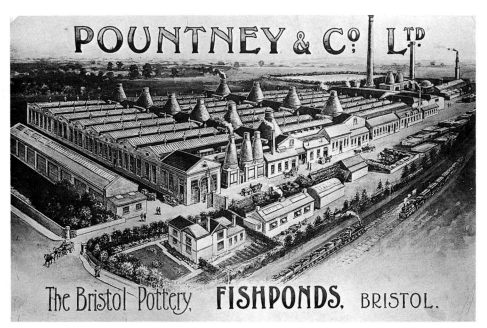

POUNTNEY & C? L?D

The Bristol Pottery, FISHPONDS, BRISTOL.

Above, advertising card, c. 1910.
BRO 20165/33. Left, tile-
making, c. 1905. *X10, 147A.*

Left, sanitary
casting
department,
c. 1950.
X10, 322A.
Below, plate-
making on hand-
operated jiggers,
c. 1928.
X10, 501A.

Handling teacups, c. 1905. *X10, 144A.*

Above, girl war-workers employed on the kilns, 1914, with their foreman. Back row, left to right, Miss Ship, Mrs Maggs, Rose Dagger, Eddie Blake, ?, Doll Trubody, Miss Taylor. Front, ?, ?, Miss Winstone. *X10, 610A. Left*, Ern Dagger unloading a tunnel oven, from the *Illustrated Bristol News*, October 1961, p. 36. *X10, 609A.*

Ern Dagger entering a biscuit oven, from the *Bristol Evening Post*, 6 February, 1954, p. 7, *X10, 608A*.

Top, Hazel Gearing and her assistants Audrey and Olive applying underglaze-transfer prints, with the Lord Mayor of Stoke-on-Trent looking on, 1959. *X10, 513A*. *Above*, underglaze paintresses with 'Tulip' on the shelves, c. 1928. Fifth from left, Betty Paddock, seventh, May Pearce, eighth, Frances Ashman. *X10, 160A*.

Top, Eva Duffett carrying a board of glazed jugs, c. 1945. *X10, 512A*. *Above*, Glost warehouse girls, c. 1905. *X10, 149A*.

Left, crate-packers, 1948. From *Moulding your child's future at the Bristol Pottery. BRO 20165/35. Below*, Betty Paddock and other paintresses dressed for a carnival, c. 1934. Betty chose 'Old Bristol Basket' as her theme because she specialised in this underglaze pattern. *X10, 482A.*

Betty Paddock, seated, demonstrating overglaze-painting at Jones' department store, Wine Street, Bristol, 1932. *X10, 481A.*

Members and supporters of the Bristol Pottery and Bovey Tracey Pottery cricket teams, 18 September 1920, with Alick Newsom seated, centre, T.B. Johnston and A.S. Adams in hats and suits standing, centre, and Patrick Johnston, then a teenager, bareheaded in a suit to the right. *X10, 320A.*

Daily life at Pountneys

One of T.B. Johnston's main concerns was to provide a better working environment. But for all the skylights and ventilators, the Pottery remained an uncomfortable workplace and many jobs continued to be hard, dangerous and unhealthy. The roofs leaked and the heating rarely worked properly; paintresses shivered through the winter and in summer worked under gloomy whitewashed windows, which were supposed to keep out the heat. The many discomforts experienced by the placers have already been described. The makers were constantly in the damp; 'Snowfire' cream and engine oil were popular remedies for chapped hands, but because the processes called for the same action over and over again a cut easily became poisoned. Accidents with machinery were also a hazard. Frederick England vividly recalled how he came by a scar on his finger:

> I had a splinter in there in 1919 in the Pottery. They had a man to do ambulance work as well as his own work. I went to him and he started to take it out and the hooters went for two minutes silence! That was the first two minutes silence after the First War. He stopped and he wouldn't do any more until the two minutes was up!

The worst problems were undoubtedly caused by clay dust. Despite regular sweeping it got everywhere and everyone seemed to have permanent coughs. The grinding mills, the making shops and the kilns were the most dangerous areas. Only the night-sweepers regularly wore masks, although caps and overalls were given out and laundered by the firm. Workers received monthly health checks, but a significant proportion contracted 'potter's rot', or silicosis. This condition, which was frequently fatal, always caused some degree of invalidity. Although Rose McAuliffe's husband organised the workers' health-checks, as a manager he did not have them himself:

> So they sent him to Radstock to have his examination with his chest, where the miners go, and I sat with him, on top of the steps, and who came up but the two doctors that he's had to deal with, with the workmen! and they said to him, 'Well hello, what are you doing here? We've never examined you on the works!'. . .and of course that's what they brought in at the inquest – 70 per cent at first, but then it advanced and it was 100 per cent, he got worse.
>
> It was terrible nursing him. . .four years. . .but in the end he didn't have enough breath to breathe, not even eat! My sister said 'I never want to see another man with it'.

35

I got 11 shillings a week for that on top of me pension, but I had never a shilling more as the pension did go up. That stopped at 11 all the time.

Such compensation had been won by the Potters' Union, which helped to prepare cases to go before Industrial Tribunals. 'They used to do a lot of good in those days. *Real* good they did because of silicosis and all that sort of thing'.[1] T.B. Johnston encouraged membership. Although over half the workforce were women, and many paid dues, the union was considered a male province. As Phyllis Creed put it, 'The women were thought of as inferior and the men just did the job'. Union representatives made trips to Stoke-on-Trent for meetings, and officials from H.Q. came down to sort out trouble. In the 1950s the placers negotiated a shorter week but were refused overtime rates for extra hours. Charles Harman saw Bert Duffett, the union 'rep':

> 'Bert', I said, 'Can you deal with the situation?' 'Not really', he said, 'Do you want me to send for Mr Tranter?'
>
> And Mr Storey, that was our accountant, cashier fellow, said, 'Oh no, we don't want any of that!' So anyway, Mr Tranter came down... He said, 'It's all right, we've had *exactly* the same case occur in another pottery' – Burslem or somewhere – 'We got time-and-a-half'. Mr Storey didn't know. So anyway, we battled. He said, 'I'll give you time-and-a-fifth... I'll give you time-and-a-quarter'...
>
> Eventually Tranter came up with his trump card: 'Well, Mr Storey, this is how they operate in Stoke, they are of the same union, they've got to have the same conditions.' He nearly went through the floor! 'I can't afford to pay that!'...but that was that solved.

The Bristol Pottery rarely experienced a strike and those they did have were usually unofficial. This was true of the industry as a whole and was probably more due to the fact that the poorly-paid workers could not afford to strike than to any lack of grievances. In the 1920s and 1930s the union's power was broken down by years of short-time working.

Wages in the industry were traditionally calculated on piecework at so-much per dozen items, but a 'dozen' might mean 12 three-pint jugs or 144 small items. Graham Tyler explained the system when he started in 1918:

> Every dozen of cups was not 12 but 36 and it was claimed that if 12 reached the packing shed in good condition that was fair play—there were losses right throughout the factory. We did 36 to the dozen. For 20 dozen you received two shillings. That was the wages in those days and my wages for 52 hours a week was ten shillings when I started... A man's wages was 27 shillings a week—that was top wages. I think the top woman's wage was about 18 shillings.

Many people left because of the pay. Mrs Cottle, an overglaze paintress, got another job in 1939:

> I liked it at the Pottery, but the money was so poor. I was 18 then and wasn't earning very much. I started at a guinea a week at Marks & Spencers. At the Pottery I started off at five-and-sixpence and sixpence of that was taken for the National Insurance. Then after six months it rose to seven-and-sixpence a week and I used to take home about seven shillings a week, so of course we couldn't get much on that. I think my mother could barely keep me on what I brought home from there.

Pountneys closed for a week each August, but holiday pay was only given from 1937. In the early days workers also had to sign on at the labour exchange when the factory closed for ten days at Christmas. From the 1920s most employees worked a 48-hour week, including Saturday mornings. The day began at seven or eight o'clock, depending on the department. People scrambled to clock-in as the factory hooter blew at five-to-seven, since late-comers were locked out for two hours and precious money would be lost.

This regulation and many others were laid down in the factory rule book. By 1959 the three-page 1940 edition had been enlarged to 12 pages. Employees were not allowed unauthorised visits to other departments. They could be fined two-and-sixpence for swearing and for throwing clay or other missiles. Persistent offenders were dismissed. Workers were reminded that, 'A fine tradition and reputation such as we have can easily be affected by a few slovenly-clothed and ill-mannered individuals.' [2]

The rule book also mentioned the Works Committee. Composed of equal numbers of employees and managers, this met monthly 'for the purpose of enhancing the working conditions and welfare of all employees'. Its first minute-book survives and gives a vivid picture of factory life in 1919. [3] The first meeting, on 5 June, discussed whether the factory ought to re-open halfway through the unpaid August holiday to allow workers to return if they so wished. This was agreed at the next meeting, and the new 'good-from-hand' payment system was discussed, which meant that workers would no longer be penalised for losses at a later stage in production. Building work had caused the male lavatories to be moved uncomfortably close to the glost-warehouse exit, much to the embarrassment of the female workers. The lack of mess-rooms was another problem:

> Mr Harvey complained that the Slip-makers had no place in which to keep their food, and consequently it got very dry. Mr Adams suggested that Miss Borton Brown might see what could be done. [4]

T.B. Johnston appointed this lady as works 'matron'. At the Works Committee's inaugural dinner he expressed appreciation:

...of the good work Miss Borton Brown had done, although she had been with us for comparatively a short time, and the work was quite new to her, as indeed it was to us also. She had, however, tackled the job in a most capable way, and he thought her influence was now apparent throughout the Works.[5]

In December 1919 she was replaced by Miss Gertrude Smith. A formidable person, she 'ran the whole roost' for the next 20 years, dealing with pay rises and recruitment, testing room temperatures and setting up keep-fit classes. She used to check the clay-end girls were not wearing damp aprons, and 'shoo' off the young paintresses when her eagle eye spotted them toasting bread around the bottle ovens;[6] 'In the winter a piece of thick bread on a three to four foot length of wire with an open kiln door throwing its tremendous heat at you is an extremely pleasant way of spending your breakfast half-hour!'[7] Matron left in the early 1940s. Harry Bryant, a sales representative who had started in the office in 1911, was then appointed personnel officer. He retired in the 1960s.

Eating on the premises was strictly forbidden, but many people had nooks and corners where they could fry-up on an oil stove or brew tea at a kiln. Others sent apprentices to collect a home-cooked dinner or a bowl of chips.

In 1920 a canteen and a mess-room were opened in three converted houses on Justice Road, next to the factory, essential parts of T.B. Johnston's great industrial plan. A recreation club was officially opened on 18 September 1920, at a cost of around £8,500. The *Pottery Gazette* described it:

> A recreation ground of an area of 11 acres... has been acquired by the company, and upon it they have built a cricket pavilion and an institute, which includes a billiard-room with two tables, reading and games rooms, skittle-alley, and football dressing- and bath-rooms, with kitchen and the necessary offices... A capable and efficient committee have been elected, who have drawn up a very well-arranged set of rules... The social side of the work as applying to the women employees will be cared for under Miss Smith... a really attractive programme of social events is being arranged for the women folk for the winter season. Next season it is hoped to extend the already-formed cricket, rambling and swimming clubs, and also physical drill, cycling, hockey, tennis, etc., the desire of the management being that the women's side should be quite as carefully looked after as the men's.[8]

The celebrations began with a cricket match between the Bristol Pottery and the Bovey Tracey Pottery, which Bristol won by 44 runs. Refreshments at Fishponds Parish Hall were followed by an entertainment. The programme listed songs by Mr Flook the works manager, Tommy Podmore the foreman glost placer, Janet Johnston and Alick Newsom, whilst Colin Linton gave a humorous recitation.[9]

The Social Club had a thriving membership until the 1960s, although the sportsground was sold in the 1930s. Hockey, tennis, bowls, skittles and cricket were regularly played:

> Anyone as could play cricket very well round here, young Mr Johnston, he'd say they could get a job in the Pottery... If you did your job ever so well it didn't make any difference; if you could play cricket it was all right![10]

The less athletic could play billiards, whist, cribbage or darts. For many years the Club was a formidable member of the Bristol Commercial House League, playing against well-known companies. Mr Harman captained the cribbage team,

> ...and we had a quiz league which I got enthusiastic about – really good fun... we used to meet some nice people: G.B. Brittons, the boot people, W.D. & H.O. Wills, the aeroplane factory and George's Brewery.

Although ladies' nights, dances and children's Christmas parties were held, the Social Club was very much a working-men's club, and young women did not take part in many formal activities. They still had plenty of fun; there were birthday treats, outings and raffles with pottery as the prize. Some gave demonstrations at local stores and wore Bristol Pottery fancy dress at carnivals. Two girls even went to the 1935 Burlington House industrial art exhibition dressed as teapots.[11]

Over half the workforce was female, and since, until the 1940s, most women were required to leave work on marriage, they were mainly teenagers or in their early 20s. Before *Music While You Work* was broadcast through the building, they used to sing all day long: 'Hours and hours. One stopped and another would start.'[12] Although some foremen and women were stern disciplinarians, the atmosphere was generally relaxed with plenty of opportunities to 'have a laugh'. The apprentice paintresses often got bored with 'Persian red':

> We had one girl start in our crowd, her name was Olive somebody and she was very tall and sunburnt with very dark skin and she had black hair that she did in two long plaits. When she was on this red she used to get it on her hands and rub her face. She looked like a Red Indian and we called her 'Minnie Ha Ha'![13]

The decorators were reputedly the prettiest girls in the factory – one was even a beauty queen:

They were lovely . . . always dressed immaculately. They came in with beautiful clothes on and they didn't have any better for Sundays than they did for weekdays, they were wearing their best all the time. It was such a clean job of course – one going on a turntable, someone else on a little clean transfer, there was no dirt whatever![14]

The cleanliness or otherwise of the different jobs created social distinctions. 'Clay-end' workers thought the paintresses and office girls considered themselves above the rest. The atmosphere in those departments was certainly never as blue as it could be elsewhere. The underglaze-transferers, usually older. women, had a particular reputation for earthiness. It was said that, one Christmas Eve in the 1930s, they trapped an unfortunate salesman and sent him home with his private parts embellished with willow pattern![15] Although many teenage girls suffered from the attentions of older men, this story is one of several showing that sexual harassment worked both ways at Pountneys.

Relationships between the men and women were generally very happy; indeed a remarkable number of marriages took place between workers. Charles Harman recounted how he met his wife, Pamela:

I was always partial to a sweet and the kiln being so dry and hot my mouth was always dry – they'd come in and I had a table where I used to keep my little ledgers, and as the girls used to go by they'd lob a sweet or something.
   The wife came to work there. She was one of these with a lovely pixie face. We got on pretty well, she was always throwing me sweets and all that and from there on it developed. We went out together and eventually married!

In the early days Pountneys would give the happy couple crockery. When Eva and Bert Duffett married, 'they had us up in the office and said we could choose anything on the factory for a wedding present. . . My husband chose a dinner-set and it was an export order that you couldn't buy in England.'

Sometimes paintresses would decorate a set for their bottom drawer. Winifred Mellor marked hers with 'Xmas 1939' under each piece. She still has a few tureens and meat dishes to remind her of her wedding day. Winifred's father was one of many craftsmen recruited from Stoke-on-Trent. Although resented by some Bristolians, the Staffordshire surnames encountered in Fishponds today show that they were appreciated by a good many local girls.

The friendly, caring environment was certainly partly due to the number of people who not only married but brought their children and relatives to work for Pountneys. The Lintons, the Blakes, the Morgans, the Daggers, the Oxenhams and many more families gave generations of service to the Bristol Pottery. They often did related jobs and so family pride was integrally connected to pride in their work. Looking back on this long tradition, which only broke down in the 1950s, Graham Tyler commented, 'I think that's what made the reputation of the firm, association of the families. . .'

NOTES

1. Smith.
2. BMAG Na1302.
3. Private collection. Copy in Bristol Museum and Art Gallery.
4. Minutes for 3.7.19.
5. Minutes for 2.6.19.
6. Creed, Roper and Thompson.
7. Bodsworth.
8. *Pottery Gazette*, October 1920, p. 1350.
9. Private collection. Copy in Bristol Museum and Art Gallery.
10. Smith.
11. Thompson.
12. England.
13. Cottle.
14. Harman.
15. Anon.

History and art: pottery 1905–1930

T.B. Johnston would have been well aware of Bristol's distinguished potting tradition. Tin-glazed earthenware had been examined as early as 1873 in Hugh Owen's *Two Centuries of Ceramic Art in Bristol*. It was supposed to have come to this country from Delft in Holland, and so it was commonly called 'delftware' by a growing band of enthusiasts. Shortly after the new factory was built, W.J. Pountney excavated the site of the 17th century Brislington Pottery. His findings were published in 1920 in *Old Bristol Potteries*, the culmination of many years' research. This interest in delftware enabled the Bristol Pottery to utilise its long history for sales purposes and claim for its own an entirely new design 'library'.

Nearly every press article referred to Pountneys' great age. The factory's printed marks, called 'backstamps', gave 1750 as the year of establishment until W.J. Pountney's book showed that the Temple Back Pottery's earliest deeds dated from 1683. The backstamp was changed accordingly. In 1914, during excavations at the Brislington site, Pountney had discovered a fragment of delftware with 1652 painted on it. This earlier date was used on backstamps after the Second World War.

In 1911 the *Pottery Gazette* reviewed an article on delftware in the *Connoisseur*, written by Richard Quick, Superintendent of Bristol Art Gallery.[1] This was followed by a description of Pountneys' new products, which had 'many of the features of early Bristol Pottery'. In 1909 the *Pottery Gazette* had illustrated one of the firm's 'Bristol delf [sic] designs in dinner ware', a tureen with a delicate scrolled border.[2] Some of Pountneys' later 'delf designs' followed the originals quite closely; 'Old Bristol 18th Century' was an underglaze-print based on a typical delftware *chinoiserie* pattern, showing an exotic bird, a willow, a zig-zag fence and a paeony. The teapots illustrated here show the pattern with overglaze-painted details and Bristol's creamy 'Amberone' glaze, introduced in the early 1920s in line with fashion.

Delftware gave lasting inspiration to Pountneys. The bright, bold patterns, painted freehand in spontaneous-looking brush-strokes, are reflected in designs throughout the factory's existence. These give Bristol pottery its own unique character and their importance cannot be too strongly emphasised.

Pountneys were also interested in the hand-painting on Bristol hard-paste porcelain of the 1770s. The 'double-ribband' pattern, with pink and blue ribbons entwined in a floral border, was reproduced by overglaze-painters from at least 1913, the date on a plate by Thomas Trafford.[3] This bears the backstamp 'REPRODUCTION OF OLD BRISTOL 1770-1781 TRAPNELL COLLECTION'. Part of the Alfred Trapnell collection is now owned by Bristol Museum and Art Gallery. Similar designs were still being painted in the 1950s. 'The Old Bristol Spray' was a lithographic transfer-print also based on Bristol hard-paste porcelain. It appears on a plate date-stamped 1919[4] and was revived 30 years later.

The celebrated painter William Fifield's lively flowers, such a feature of Bristol pottery from c.1816 to 1850, were another enduring source of inspiration, although a specific pattern may not have been copied until 1952; an article in *Pottery and Glass* illustrated a dish from a set painted by Fifield for Bristol's Mansion House in 1828 and a 'Reproduction of the Fifield pattern produced in 1952 specially for the dollar markets'.[5]

Freehand painting had fallen out of fashion after Fifield's death and the general standard of decoration at the Bristol Pottery declined with its fortunes. The Arts and Crafts movement saw a revival of interest in hand-work, coupled with a new enthusiasm for historical patterns. Pountneys had some awareness of contemporary trends; a painted plate from the 1880s[6] echoes the style of the ceramicist William de Morgan. By the early 20th century the once *avant-garde* Arts and Crafts ideas had been absorbed into popular taste. T.B. Johnston set out to reintroduce hand-painting at Pountneys in response to a widespread demand for 'art-wares'.

The hand-painting revival of the early 20th century was made possible by an abundance of cheap labour which continued until the Second World War. Employment and training opportunities were still very limited in most industries, and so there was no shortage of girls with an artistic flair, ready to take up a seemingly attractive occupation. The Bristol paintresses had been used to filling in printed patterns and painting simple bands and lines, but they would have been less able to tackle complex subjects. Whilst the paintresses learnt as they went along, the few male trainees, like Cecil Garland and Charlie Smith, were encouraged to attend evening art classes, and particular attention was given to them by several highly-trained 'artists' recruited from rival potteries. These were men who understood fashionable styles elsewhere in the industry and their example helped to raise the general standard of work.

The move to Fishponds substantially increased production and new members of staff had been taken on in preparation. William Moore Binns, appointed art director in 1904 after a distinguished career at Royal Worcester, was possibly Johnston's greatest 'catch', although he only stayed a short time. Johnston was particularly attracted by the underglaze-painted Wemyss ware with its bold designs of fruit, flowers and birds, made by the Fife Pottery in Scotland. At least two Wemyss artists, David Grinton and George Stewart, worked at Bristol.[7]

43

Stewart, who trained at Wedgwood, came as part of a 'package-deal'; Pountneys bought the reproduction rights to several Wemyss patterns and needed someone to paint them. Charlie Smith remembered Stewart as a colourful character:

> When he was up in Scotland they sent a photograph of all the river and all the boats going up. He said 'What a wonderful place!... Instead of that I'm in a stinking hole!'

Comical Wemyss-ware cats decorated with naturalistic pink roses are avidly collected today. Stewart taught his apprentices to paint this rose. Charlie Smith and Cecil Garland continued to do so until the factory closed. Like many of his pieces, a vase painted with Wemyss-type fruit is stamped in black with his initials. An inscription states that it was made from the first clay produced at Fishponds, in April 1905. Stewart painted another Wemyss pattern, with black cocks and hens strutting along the grass. Pountneys marketed this under the backstamp, 'The Bristol "Cock & Hen" Pottery', giving the impression that it came from a tiny workshop rather than one of the biggest potteries in Europe. The 'cock and hen' theme was further elaborated in a range backstamped 'The Bristol Fiscal Pottery'. The birds represented Joseph Chamberlain chasing Campbell Bannerman. A verse underneath probably referred to the General Election of 1905. Johnston was a keen supporter of Chamberlain's campaign for trade protection. 'The Bristol "Cat & Dog" Pottery' was yet another range painted by Stewart, featuring designs by the well-known cartoonist Louis Wain.

Samuel Shufflebotham, who was born in 1875 in Leek, near Stoke-on-Trent, worked at Bristol from c.1900 to 1929 apart from 1908 to 1915, when he went to work at the Llanelli Pottery. Interestingly, 'Shuff' was remembered there as an accomplished imitator of Wemyss, although he was probably taught the style at Bristol.[8] The Bristol speciality developed by him, sometimes sold under the name 'The Bristol Leaded Lights Pottery', was a series of Puritan-type heads representing Englishmen, Irishmen, Scotsmen, Germans and Americans, often shown against a segmented background resembling leaded glass. Each had a hand-written motto, such as 'There's mair in the kitchen'.[9] Similar designs were painted by Shufflebotham at Llanelli.

These mottoes are reminiscent of those found on Torquay ware. Shufflebotham actually moved to Torquay in 1929, and subsequently worked for the Crown Dorset Pottery. Torquay pottery has much in common with Bristol's hand-painted products.[10] Wemyss-type roses and cocks and hens are often depicted. So too are diving kingfishers which were a favourite of Thomas Trafford, who worked for Pountneys from the 1890s to the 1930s as an overglaze artist and print designer. The

'Sandringham' pattern with blue and white Renaissance-type scrolls, made at Torquay from the late 19th century, could easily be the prototype for Bristol's best-selling 'Blue Scroll', painted from the 1930s onwards. The distinctive Torquay style was also produced at nearby Bovey Tracey. It is perhaps significant that T.B. Johnston also owned the main Bovey Tracey Pottery. When the Fife Pottery closed in 1930 he gave its chief decorator a job at Bovey Tracey and Wemyss ware was made there until 1957.[11]

Further inspiration for Bristol's early art-wares was to be found only a few miles from Fishponds, at Sir Edmund Elton's Sunflower Pottery at Clevedon Court. Pountneys made close copies of Elton's unusual vases with their streaky glazes and crackled gold effects.[12]

Mainstream products

Art-wares represented only a small proportion of the Bristol Pottery's output, which included tableware, toilet-ware and kitchen-ware, usually with printed designs chosen to have the widest commercial appeal. Johnston also strove for good workmanship in these areas; for instance, in 1895 he recruited Ernest Styche from the Royal Worcester factory, who became head engraver at Fishponds. However neither the shapes nor the patterns were outstandingly different from those sold by other potteries.

Although earthenware could never compete with top-quality bone china, Pountneys tried to make it seem as good. From the 1890s many Bristol earthenware items had 'semi-porcelain' or 'semi-china' on their backstamps. The 1909 *Pottery Gazette* article mentioned another earthenware body:

> It is hard fired, and is almost as light as china. The peculiar whiteness of 'Alkalon' is especially suitable for dinner ware, and there are several new designs in dinner sets with neat patterns printed in a very pleasing shade of flown green. . . A very pleasing dinner service is in 'antique' shape, with 'Odelberg' design.[13]

'Odelberg' was an underglaze-printed *Art Nouveau* design in a muted blue-green. 'Flown' colours were specially treated to give a soft, slightly blurred effect. A catalogue in Bristol Museum and Art Gallery lists 'Odelberg's' wholesale price as from plain printed at 6/9d for a 26-piece set to 30/1d for a 70-piece set with gilding and extra painted colours.[14] Most of the printed patterns were vaguely *rococo*, an ornate style popular for generations, or the more recent *Art Nouveau*, or perennial favourites like willow pattern or tiny pink rosebuds.

Not only were different permutations of patterns sold, but also the range of designs was considerably wider than would be the case today.

45

This was probably because the main customers were small retailers rather than chain-stores, and labour was cheap. The Pottery even carried out individual commissions, with no guarantee that they would be profitable. In 1924 local businessman Ernest Huntley was setting up home in Redland, Bristol, with his wife Rosie, and they ordered from Pountneys a large dinner-service printed in gold on a rich mottled blue. They were later told that this special order would never be repeated since an entire set had had to be rejected and smashed before the exact colour was achieved.[15]

Tableware was made in far more shapes than would be considered economic today. The above-mentioned catalogue illustrated eight different dinner-ware shapes and six teacups. The creation of a new shape is a major investment; if it fails, a great deal of money is lost but if customers like it then it will remain in production for many years.

NOTES

1. *Pottery Gazette*, November 1911, p. 1236.
2. *Pottery Gazette*, June 1909, pp. 679–80.
3. Prudential auction rooms, Weston-super-Mare, 26 April, 1988: Lot 123.
4. BMAG N9405.
5. *Pottery and Glass*, July 1952, p. 54.
6. BMAG N8576.
7. I am grateful to Harry Frost for information about William Moore Binns. Peter Davis and Robert Rankine, *Wemyss Ware, a decorative Scottish Pottery*, Scottish Academic Press, 1986, p. 25, for Grinton.
8. Ibid, p. 33. I am grateful to David Pugh and Gareth Hughes for information about Samuel Shufflebotham.
9. BMAG Loan 78/163.
10. See D. and E. Lloyd Thomas, *The Old Torquay Potteries*, Arthur H. Stockwell Ltd., Ilfracombe, 1977.
11. Davis and Rankine, loc. cit.
12. See Malcolm Haslam, *Elton Ware; the Pottery of Sir Edmund Elton*, Richard Dennis, Shepton Beauchamp, Somerset, 1989.
13. *Pottery Gazette*, loc. cit.
14. BMAG NX1188.
15. BMAG Loan 90/13.

Left to right: Bristol hard-paste porcelain plate with painted 'double-ribband' pattern, c. 1775, *G497*. Lemonade jug, 'Lord Nelson' shape, overglaze-painted by Albert Pollard for George VI's coronation, 1937, *Na1130*. Plate, marked 'Bristol 1770–1781', 'The Old Bristol Spray' overglaze-printed pattern, 1953, *Na1324*.

Shaped dish from a service made by the Bristol Pottery and painted by William Fifield for Bristol's Mansion House, c. 1828, *N9061*. Soup dish, c. 1952, *Na190*. Both overglaze-printed and hand-coloured.

Underglaze-printed dinner-wares: Tureen, cover and stand, 'Ashton' 1919, *Na543*. Plates, left to right, 'Emerson' 1914, *N9379*, 'Sutherland' 1910, 'Odelberg' c. 1920.

Left to right: Jar and cover stamped GS for George Stewart, 1922, *Na1044*. Toilet-boxes, stamped 'HANDWORK', 1929/1930, *Na608*. Dish, marked 'Decoration by The Bristol Porcelain Painters, 1750–19(23) The Bristol Pottery ENG.', *Na1330*. Vases, marked 'Bristol Gold Crackle', 1918, *Na602*, and 1921, *Na1043*.

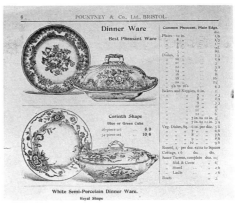

Catalogue, c. 1920, *NX1188*.

Winifred Mellor, overglaze paintress, poses with George V Silver Jubilee mugs for distribution to Bristol schoolchildren. 1935. *X10, 617A*.

'Dorland' shapes designed by J.F. Price, with underglaze 'banding-and-lining': Tureen and cover, *Na192*. Soup bowl and stand, *Na377*. c. 1935.

'Burlington' shape dinner-service, designed by J.F. Price, with overglaze print. *Na1027–Na1031*, 1939.

Underglaze-printing with overglaze-painted details, left to right: 'Summertime' pattern cup and saucer, c. 1930. 'Academy' shape plate, 'Waterlily' pattern, 1936, *Na1075*. 'Dorland' shape tureen, cover and stand, 'Newlyn' pattern, 1936. 'Academy' shape coffee-pot, 'Campden' pattern, 1937.

Badge-ware, underglaze-printed with banding-and-lining, 1930–1960: Coffee-cup and saucer, *Na945*. Coffee-cups, 'The Grand Central Hotel', 'Watts & Co. Limited', 'Sunshine Hotel', 'La Plage Hotel', 'La Speranza' and National Petrol Company logo. Bristol Corporation plate, *NX1189*. Blaise Mansion Café plate, *NX1190*.

Catalogue of kitchen-ware designed by J.F. Price, c. 1938. *BRO 20165/34.*

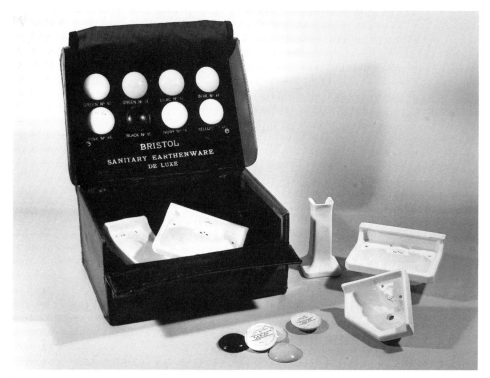

Sample case with models of sanitary castings and glazed discs showing available colours. c. 1935.

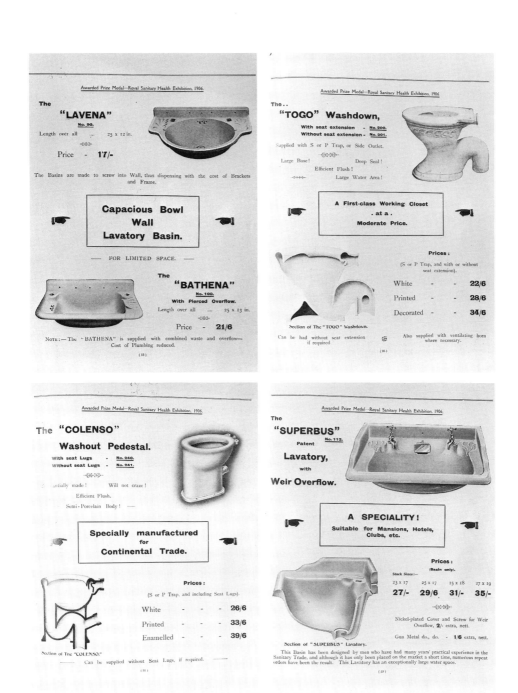

Sanitary castings catalogues c. 1910, *BRO 20165/25/26/27*.

The Queen and glost placers inside a bottle oven. *X10, 483A.*

Bristol Pottery's firewatch party in front of the lodge, c. 1943. Seated, left to right, Charlie Smith, Patrick Johnston, Arthur Adams, Alick Newsom. *X10, 842A.*

Queen Mary's visit, 1941. The Queen examines a bowl with Patrick Johnston in the showroom. 'Burlington' and 'Academy' are in the background, and a figure of Winston Churchill stands in front of them. Patrick Johnston wore a hearing-aid. *X10, 324A.*

Form and function: pottery from the 1930s

The hand-crafted look was modified in the 1930s under the influence of the rectilinear functional modernism promoted by German and Swedish designers. A concern for 'good design' was so widely felt that a series of industrial art exhibitions attracted crowds of visitors.

One of the most significant events in the history of the Fishponds factory was the appointment of J.F. Price as consultant designer in 1933. Although Johnston carefully nurtured the firm's art-wares, the lack of a talented hand was clearly apparent in its more utilitarian designs. Jack Price brought a new vitality with his 'Modern Bristol' shapes. Named after the Dorland House exhibition of 1933 and the Royal Academy exhibition, held at Burlington House in 1935, they were recognised as some of the most exciting products of the British ceramic industry. 'Dorland', a strongly *Art Deco* design, featured three little feet on cylindrical coffee-pots and hemispherical tureens, whilst 'Burlington' had solid rings as bases; 'Academy' was another cylindrical shape.

Price also created a range of kitchen-ware. Again, it was carefully designed with the needs of the modern kitchen in mind. A contemporary brochure shows a housewife taking a handled storage jar with its air-tight lid from her up-to-the-minute kitchenette unit and pouring her ingredients from a conical easy-to-read measuring cup into a non-splash whisking bowl. All the items came in fashionable apple-green or primrose, undecorated apart from 'BARLEY', 'PRUNES' or suchlike in bold capitals on the jars.[1] Price's measuring-jug and jars were such good shapes that they were still being made in the 1960s.

Jack Price and T.B. Johnston were in many ways quite similar. Although less stout, Price was 'a formidable figure who looked rather like Henry VIII'.[2] Both were extremely able, with strong personalities and boundless energy. They shared a passion for politics, but there the similarity stopped since Price was deeply involved in the Labour movement. He had been art director at the Royal Cauldon factory in Stoke-on-Trent, but went freelance when the firm ran into financial difficulties. He worked for the ceramic-fireplace manufacturers Thynnes of Hereford as well as Pountneys until his death at the age of 40 in 1943.

In a lecture given to the Design and Industries Association in 1947, Alick Newsom summed up Price's importance for Bristol:

> Little interesting can be said about the early part of this century, and it was not until the late J.F. Price joined us in 1933 . . . that we really woke up from a somewhat restless sleep. His influence launched us, I readily believe, into a new era, both in the realm of shapes as well as

designs. Price had a profound influence on the two particular trades with which he had a lot to do – tiles and domestic pottery... At Bristol he first designed for us a new shape, with which some of you will be familiar. This was first produced in 1935, and was at once successful, though I had some qualms about the feet of the vegetable dishes, both as to factory losses, and also as to possible complaints from customers. Fortunately, however, neither materialised, and the venture was a complete success. You see, it works well at home, decorates well and consequently, in spite of its unusual shape, sells well. Being shown first at the Dorland Hall Exhibition, we gave it the name Dorland. Price also did for us, a little later, another modern shape in contrast to the first one, it is easier to pot, again works well at home, and, though not quite so easy to decorate, it sells well.

Then – alas – he died in 1943, having worked himself to death. He never seemed to stop working. He was either writing, reading, drawing or lecturing us on the advantages of being a Communist, finally contracted T.B. and just burnt himself up, poor fellow. He was undoubtedly a genius and we and our friends at Hereford miss him more than I can say.[3]

Price, working closely with Cecil Garland, also raised the standard of decoration at Pountneys. He exploited its tradition of hand-painting to the full, transforming its exuberant flowers into a style which fulfilled all the requirements of 'good design'. The rhythmic brush-strokes of simple stylised motifs showed a new understanding of the old delftware techniques.

Many firms made hand-painted pottery in the 1930s. Bristol pottery is comparatively unknown today, but its best hand-painting is easily comparable with some of the most sought-after products of Stoke-on-Trent. Bristol paintresses particularly excelled at 'banding-and-lining', in which bands of graduated colour and width were juxtaposed to form a deep border. This technique, a development of the traditional plain line around rims, enjoyed widespread popularity in the 1930s. It was particularly suited to modern shapes, such as 'Dorland'. The 'excellent banding and lining' was singled out for praise by one journalist in a review of the 1935 'British Art in Industry' exhibition at the Royal Academy:

> ...banding is a new thing, and that is what we surely need, a *principle* of ornament for modern pottery... It arises in the fundamentals of ceramic process... It satisfies our present demand for relevance and for abstraction, but it has immense possibilities of artistic design. It admits transitional, contrasted, combined and complementary colours, and it makes the highest demands on colour sense in pottery chemists and designers... Its permutations... are an instrument which only potters who are artists can use in the higher degrees, but which every potter can pleasantly employ.[4]

Banding-and-lining depended on the skill of the practitioner rather than the designer. Indeed while Cecil Garland created many complicated hand-painted patterns, he never designed the deceptively simple-looking borders because he could not achieve the same proficiency as the paintresses who did banding-and-lining day in and day out. In this area the girls reigned supreme. They worked out the carefully graduated colours on trial plates, in their own time, and the best would be kept for reference. If a customer liked one it would go into production. Although the paintresses were not paid for their ideas, there was a great deal of satisfaction in recognising one's own design. Phyllis Creed once went into the Tralee Hotel at Weston-super-Mare and was delighted to recognise her own work on the tables. It was also satisfying to develop a high degree of skill. Phyllis Creed was once told by a delegation from Wedgwood that they had never seen lines as fine as hers, and they offered her a job! Although simple edging lines are still commonly hand-painted, complex banding-and-lining went out of fashion in the 1950s.

The modern painted designs were fairly expensive and catered for a particular sort of middle-class, educated consumer; Heals of Tottenham Court Road sold several of Pountneys' more 'arty' ranges and so did the Bristol Guild of Applied Art. Printed wares appealed to a more traditional market. Pountneys continued to produce underglaze transfer-prints of popular subjects such as their 'Willow Pattern', 'Mallard' and 'Thames Scenes' patterns, as well as bringing the time-honoured floral border up-to-date in designs like 'Waterlily', with tiny stylised flowers. Complex coloured and shaded patterns were possible with overglaze lithographic transfers. These ranged from crinoline-ladies to crisp *Art Déco* patterns in the *Odéon* cinema idiom. Pountneys were still making some of their own 'lithos' and they were one of the few firms praised for them by Nikolaus Pevsner in *An Enquiry into Industrial Art in England* of 1937.[5]

Two new shapes were produced on more traditional lines than the 'Modern Bristol' range. 'Boston', introduced in the *Pottery Gazette* in January 1934,[6] was a rounded form very like a well-known Wedgwood shape. This elegant classic was still very much in line with current taste in the 1950s, but the hexagonal 'Shirley' was only made for a few years.

NOTES

1. BRO 20165/34.
2. I am grateful to Gordon and Irene Hopwood for information about J.F. Price.
3. *Pottery and Glass*, May 1947, p. 26.
4. *Pottery Gazette*, February 1935, p. 223.
5. Nikolaus Pevsner, *An Enquiry into Industrial Art in England*, Cambridge University Press, 1937, p. 80.
6. *Pottery Gazette*, January 1934, p. 55.

Wash-basins and corporation dinner-services: Pountneys' other products

Sanitary castings

In 1909 the *Pottery Gazette* noted:

> The company are manufacturers of high-class, non-crazing, semi-porcelain sanitary ware, including sanitary basins, pedestal closets &c. Pountney & Co., Ltd., have laid themselves out to cater for the highest grade of sanitary articles. Their 'Superbus' lavatory (patent), and the 'Bathena' wall lavatory are being specified in all quarters by architects and other specialists competent to judge of the superior merits claimed on behalf of these exclusive models. The brilliancy of the glaze in no small measure enhances the firm's reputation as manufacturers. We understand the firm are always willing to consider the question of modelling any new designs submitted to them, whether for use in hospitals, hotels, schools, railways, steamships, &c.[1]

Pountneys had only been making sanitary castings for four years, but already in 1906 they had been awarded a prize medal in the Royal Sanitary Health Exhibition. Three catalogues from this time illustrate the diversity of water-closets and sinks made for every type of market.[2] The earliest, with 'WILL NOT CRAZE' alongside every item, depicted their special 'Superbus' lavatory, a word then used for wash-basins, 'Suitable for Mansions, Hotels, Clubs, etc.'. The most expensive version cost 46/- wholesale, at a time when the average male wage was just over one pound a week. The basin was:

> . . .designed by men who have had many years' practical experience in the Sanitary Trade, the great feature being that the sides and panelling of the Basin are considerably sloped, and moreover all mouldings are rounded, thus making it impossible for any Soap, Scum, or Dirty Water to lodge thereon. . .
>
> Further, this Basin is constructed with a combined overflow – the holes in the earthenware grid being vertical, and large enough to admit of a brush for occasional cleansing purposes.
>
> To show our good faith in the merits of this particular Basin, we are prepared to send a sample, carriage paid, and on approval, to any *bona-fide* merchant.

Lavatory-pans, known as 'washdown pedestals', were made in the 'Togo' and 'Colossal' patterns and the 'Colenso', 'Specially manufactured for Continental Trade', which flushed at the front. There was even a shape for squatting, for export to India and South Africa, called the 'Hindi or Bombay Hopper'.

Although sanitary castings represented a large proportion of the firm's output, wash-basins and lavatories tend to be replaced and thrown-out. As a result, few survive. However a set of miniature samples from the 1930s shows that the shapes had hardly changed since 1909, although, as a concession to fashion, the customer could have them in black, pale green, blue, pink or primrose.

This department was to some extent assured of its market since the cost of transporting heavy items meant that builders were unlikely to patronise any firm more than 100 miles away. By the motorway era this was not such a consideration; in the 1960s Pountneys faced increasing competition from 'sanitary giants' like Twyfords. By then rival firms were promoting smooth-contoured suites, but Pountneys were slow to respond to new bathroom trends and only ever produced one streamlined model.

Hotel ware

The Bristol Pottery was also an important producer of crockery for hotels, hospitals and similar institutions. This type of ware is made with thick sides and rounded edges for strength. A special, truly 'vitreous' earthenware is often used, fired to a very high temperature so that the clay particles are fused together like glass. However Pountneys did not have the right kilns to produce a real vitreous body, and so, around 1905, the firm developed its own recipe for a strong earthenware which could be fired at a lower temperature. The 1909 *Pottery Gazette* article described the new body:

> Produced after a long series of experiments which have proved conclusively that it will stand the extremes of heat and cold to which this class of goods is liable. The body is vitrified and non-absorbent, so that if 'chipped', the surrounding parts do not discolour.[3]

'Vitrite', cunningly named to associate it with real vitreous earthenware, was a great success and the trademark appeared on backstamps until the 1960s.

Heavy-duty crockery was less subject to changing fashion than ordinary domestic tableware. Huge contracts were supplied to government departments, shipping lines and other companies. Moreover, customers were likely to return for many years; the Pottery's sales representative would encourage them to have a personalised monogram or crest on every item and so they always had to come back for replacements.

Pountneys had a vast library of these 'badges', mostly designed by Reg Hanks. He thought up a suitable motif, sent the customer a pencil drawing on a special printed card for approval, then engraved it. A few chance survivals of his later copper-plates show that Pountneys' clients ranged from the Australian Air Force and the Compañía de Navegación

Golfo Azul of South America to the Hotel Casablanca on Jersey and the Tally Ho! café.[4] As a *Bristol Evening Post* journalist commented in 1954:

> Even if you have not got any Bristol pottery in your home it is highly likely that you have used some while on holiday or when dining out, for Pountney and Co. is easily one of the biggest producers of hotel and café ware in the country... Collectors of cups and saucers with hotel crests upon them would have a field day at the Bristol Potteries. Here they will find thousands of pieces of crockery stamped with the names of famous hotels, catering establishments and holiday camps.[5]

Pountneys were said to have supplied every hotel in south-west England. Seaside customers included Brighton Corporation, which regularly ordered 600 dozen teacups a year. Pountneys' crockery even graced the tables of the *Queen Mary*.

In March 1956, Bristol Corporation bought a 5,000-piece dinner-service for the new Council House. The design, selected from 12 submitted by Cecil Garland, had an overglaze-printed and hand-coloured border, 'best gold' rims and the city crest. The *Bristol Evening Post* listed the people who decorated it:

> First there is the printer Frank Podmore. From pieces of hand-engraved copper and steel, he prints the coat-of-arms and leaf border on to paper – and supervises its transfer on to the china.
>
> Then the painters take over: Mrs Queenie Nicholls, who has been at the Pottery 14 years, and Mrs Eileen Perry, who has been there 10 years. With sure hands, they apply the leaf border and add the gold edging... The gold they are using on this job costs about £100 a kilo – but their hands never slip. 'It's quite easy once you get used to it,' says Mrs Perry... Admitting this is the most important work she has ever done, she adds: 'But I wouldn't like it in my kitchen. It's too expensive. I should be afraid of breaking it.'
>
> Painted, the pieces are 'fired'. The gold, previously a rich, brownish colour, comes out pale brown. Mrs Edith Cullimore sets to with silver sand and burnishes the gold until it glitters – to chip it she would have to chip the plate... Surrounded by all the glittering plates, cups, and pots, she says: 'I imagine it will look very nice when the tables are laid and the lights are on and catch the gold'... She pauses, and adds: 'And think of the wonderful meals that will be eaten off this set one day. I must say I would like a chance to eat off it myself. It would be a real pleasure.'[6]

Badges were usually applied under the glaze, to protect them from countless knives and forks. Short runs would be printed from flat plates whilst larger contracts were roller-printed:

> Application of badges isn't as easy as you would imagine. They had to

be put on straight and all the same distance from the edge of a plate, otherwise the job was a mess. The ware was marked up by a junior using a pencil and a little template.[7]

After printing, coloured borders were added. These sometimes had a practical function since crockery from different units such as wards or platoons needed to be distinguishable within large organisations.

From around 1966, Pountneys made a lot of promotional wares for breweries and cigarette companies; 125,000 Watneys' Red Barrel pub ashtrays were once supplied in a single order. This work was considerably more profitable than badge ware, hitherto regarded as the company's bread-and-butter. Institutional contracts were usually won by tender, which had the effect of keeping prices low and the trade fiercely competitive. In the 1960s a wholesaler for the high street market might pay four times as much as a hotel distributor for a plate that represented exactly the same amount of work. Pountneys stopped making hotel ware for this reason when they moved to Cornwall.

Other heavy-duty wares

Not all heavy-duty ware was ordinary crockery; the Pottery had contracts for Jeyes' toilet-paper holders and the first Goblin 'teasmades'. Bedpans, slop-pails and commode pans were made in great quantities. Ruby Liddington remembered seeing a consignment of urinals for a Monmouthshire hospital picked out by a junior warehouse girl:

> This was checked by the foreman, the girl who had done the order (all duly dusted of course), and the packer ready with his trolley. The foreman didn't think it at all funny on finding 144 mixed up urinals instead of six dozen male and six dozen female. The poor shattered girl nearly burst into tears and said 'Which is which? I didn't know the difference! Urinals is urinals aren't they?'!

NOTES

1. *Pottery Gazette*, June 1909, pp. 679–80.
2. BRO 20165/25–27.
3. *Pottery Gazette*, June 1909, p. 680.
4. BMAG Na1313, Na1315.
5. *Bristol Evening Post*, 6 February, 1954, p. 7.
6. Ibid, 6 March, 1956, p. 8.
7. Newsom.

'Old Bristol 18th Century' teapots, c. 1930. Underglaze-printed delftware-type *Chinoiserie* pattern with overglaze hand-painted details and 'Amberone' glaze. Large teapot, *Na1166*.

Wemyss-inspired underglaze-painted pottery, c. 1905–1925. *Left to right*: 'Fruit' vase, inscribed 'Manufactr*d* From the first Clay Made at Fishponds April 1905', and stamped GS. Dish, stamped 'POUNTNEY'S BRISTOL "COCK & HEN" POTTERY' and stamped GS. Plate, inscribed 'The Bristol "Fiscal" Pottery'. Tankard, inscribed 'The Bristol "Cat & Dog" Pottery', and stamped 'MADE AT FISHPONDS NR. BATH FOR TREADWIN DOBBS BATH'. All painted by George Stewart. Spill-jar, stamped 'BRISTOL "LEADED LIGHTS" POTTERY JA', in a style probably created by Samuel Shufflebotham.

Underglaze-painted plates, *left to right*: 'Bellflower', designed by J.F. Price, 1940. Pattern exhibited at the 'Britain Can Make It' exhibition, 1946, and the 'Festival of Britain', 1951, *Na1085*. 'Passion flower', designed and painted by Frances Ashman, marked 'REPRODUCTION OF OLD BRISTOL DELFT,' c. 1950, *Na1086*.

Delftware charger, 'tulip'-type pattern, probably Bristol, c. 1720, *N6700*. Punch-bowl, 'Fazackerly'-type pattern, Liverpool, c. 1750, *N3242*. Both designs were closely copied by Pountneys.

Top: 'Shirley' shape
dinner- and tea-items,
with overglaze-
printing, 1933.
Left: Plate underglaze-
painted in the Wemyss
style. Inscribed
'C.J. GARLAND NRD',
c. 1955, *Na1335*.

'Academy' shape coffee-service, designed by J.F. Price, with underglaze-painting, c. 1935, *Na1046*.

Top: 'Blue Scroll' plate, underglaze-painted by Charlie Smith. Pattern exhibited at the 'Britain Can Make It' exhibition, 1946, *N9260*. *Bottom*: Oven-to-tableware with sprayed colour and overglaze-printed 'Old Bristol Delft' pattern, closely copied from an 18th-century delftware design. Designed by Honor Elliot, 1963, *NX940–NX942*.

Plaque, underglaze-painted by Charlie Smith to commemorate the Pottery's fire-watch, c. 1944, *Na428*.

Underglaze-painting by Frances Ashman from the 1950s: Jug, 'Gadroon' shape, marked 'REPRODUCTION OLD BRISTOL DELFT A.D. 1652-1780', *Na958*. Plate, marked 'Made for Heals by the Bristol Pottery England', *Na952*. Dish, a close copy of the 18th–century delftware 'Fazackerly' pattern.

Advertisement for Cauldon Bristol Potteries (Cornwall) Ltd, *Tableware International*, September 1972, p. 81.

Managing without 'TB': 1938–1961

Towards the end of his life T.B. Johnston was bedridden, but continued to work from home until his death at the age of 73 in February 1938. He left the firm in the hands of his son, Patrick Bertram Gwinnell Johnston, and his nephew Alick S. Newsom. They became joint managing directors along with Arthur Adams. Mr Adams, who had been the commercial manager before becoming company secretary, relinquished his daily responsibilities in 1950, aged 85, after 71 years with the firm, but continued to keep an avuncular eye on things as director. Although concerned for his workers he drove a hard bargain, arguing against pension schemes, five-day weeks and similar new-fangled ideas.[1]

William George Cottrell, who had joined Pountneys in 1901, replaced Mr Adams as company secretary and joint managing director. In the 1930s, as sales manager, he used to drive a bus converted into a showroom. He retained his involvement in sales and, in the 1950s, made numerous promotional trips abroad.

'Master Pat', or 'PBJ', had known many workers since boyhood, when he played for the company cricket team and trailed after his father around the factory. He was profoundly deaf and this sometimes made him seem aloof, but he was liked and respected and made a point of knowing his workforce. Eva Duffett commented:

> We'd grown up with the old management. Pat Johnston, he was the same age as me and I can remember when he was 21 and I was 21, you know, and we could talk to them. . .like talking to you. . .there weren't no swank or nothing like that.

He had worked in most departments and had attended Stoke-on-Trent Technical College. His main concern was design; 'Pat's people', in the decorating departments, worked directly under him. His own work was exhibited at the 1935 Burlington House exhibition and recommended by the Design Centre in 1959.[2]

Alick Newsom came to Pountneys as a dashing young army officer in 1919. He trained as a professional serviceman, but after the First World War he accepted one of the gratuities available to officers prepared to give up their commission. Johnston, an uncle on his mother's side, offered him a job, perhaps remembering how his own uncle had invited him to join Pountneys so many years before. Alick Newsom threw himself whole-heartedly into his new career. Like Patrick Johnston, he would always help out in an emergency; they are remembered working shoulder to shoulder with the placers, stripped to the waist, desperately emptying a bottle oven against the clock. Once in later years, when an overhanging pot on a tunnel-kiln truck put a whole firing in jeopardy, Mr Newsom got out his rifle and blasted it away. Newsom was 'a charming man', 'a real gentleman', who 'had a smile for everybody'. He also had a bowl of hyacinths for a poorly office junior, and seats in his jeep to take Ern Dagger and Tom Cooksey fishing.[3]

Before the new management could make their mark, war was declared and factory life transformed. In 1939 production for the home market was restricted to encourage exports, and from 1941, under the 'Utility' scheme, all crockery for British consumption had to be undecorated. Tableware was still needed for hospitals and the armed forces, and the Bristol Pottery was designated an 'essential works'. Many of its employees were therefore in reserved occupations and so were not called up. A few decorators worked on export orders and banding-and-lining pottery for government contracts. One tunnel kiln ran on gas from the company's own plant and so production was rarely disrupted. Although 40,000 plates a week were made for the army, most of the huge factory was used as a government store.

Before air-raid shelters were built, the remaining workers would dive into the disused bottle ovens when the sirens sounded; a thick layer of glaze, accumulated over many years' firing, made them very strong. Inside they would sit on the saggars, talk, knit and generally have fun. Once, a plane came down on Fishponds playing fields, hitting the top of a kiln: 'We were safe enough, but there was a loud bang!'[4]

Union records for 1943 list 33 members on active service and a factory photograph from 1942 shows many 'home front' uniforms.[5] Phyllis Creed was an ambulance girl and Mr Newsom was second-in-command of a Home Guard battalion. Charlie Smith, who had trained with the fire-brigade before the war, was in charge of the factory's fire-watch. This patrolled 24 hours a day and maintained its own fire-pump.

The great event of the war years was undoubtedly Queen Mary's visit in 1941, which called for frantic preparations:

> Just before they came on to the works all the week before they were whitewashing and painting and all this and doing that, and she wandered in all the places that hadn't been done.[6]
> ...they hid a lot of things from her like toilet pans, water bottles and bed pans and she went straight into that room![7]

Frances Ashman remembered Queen Mary's deep voice as she looked over her shoulder and said, 'Those are very nice bowls you are doing!' Others were invited to join her for tea in the canteen and had more time to talk. Miss Aline Hibbs, chief telephonist for as long as many people could remember, treasured a cigarette the Queen gave her. A more substantial memento, preserved in the company museum, was a special plaque which she signed in gold. Bert Duffett glazed seven before he was satisfied that the surface was fit for a queen to write on.

With peace came the pressing need to reconstruct the country's damaged economy, but the loss of so many soldiers brought a serious labour shortage. Pountneys had issued a recruitment leaflet as early as 1943, hoping to lure school-leavers away from the more glamorous-sounding munitions work. After the war a more ambitious brochure, *Moulding your child's future at the Bristol Pottery*,[8] listed the advantages of working at Fishponds: the industry's new pay structure brought 'wages into favourable comparison with those of any other industry', it was a 'pleasant and interesting occupation', with *Music While You Work* and a work-bench tea service, but most of all, 'a potter's work gives the pride and satisfaction that come to a skilled craftsman making things with his own hands' and, 'The goods we make go to all markets of the world, and you can be proud in the knowledge that you are helping in the trade recovery of your country'. About this time the rule that women should leave work when they married was finally dropped. Former employees were invited back and part-time hours for mothers became common.

A number of improvements were made in the late 1940s, although *Pottery and Glass* noted in 1948 that, 'the extent of recent development' had been, 'less spectacular than is the case with some of the Potteries firms'.[9] It went on to describe the new roller-conveyors installed alongside the remaining bottle ovens. Their slight gradient allowed saggars to slide along to where the girls could empty them in comfort and the saggars were no longer carried out one by one. This system was to be short-lived, since the two continuously-fired tunnel kilns, installed in 1938, were augmented by another electric tunnel kiln in 1953. An oil-fired biscuit kiln, built in 1957, completed the company's transition from bottle ovens. Some were demolished to provide more flexible work spaces. Pountneys were particularly proud of a vast hall which housed the glost tunnel kiln, the cranking department, in which ware was stacked on trolleys ready for the kilns, and the glost sorters who took it off at the other end.

In 1948 two semi-automatic making machines replaced some of the old hand-operated jolleys and jiggers, so that the profile tool which shaped cups and plates was brought down mechanically. With new equipment Ray Wood could now make a complete jug in two minutes: 25 dozen a day.

In the late 1950s a 'Murray Curvex' print-transferring machine was installed for flat items; a convex rubber pad was bumped onto the plate, stamping down the pattern. This did away with tissue transfers. However the old method was still needed for more complicated shapes and so the transferers' art was not lost. Screen-printing was another new development widely adopted by the pottery industry in the 1950s, a cheaper method of producing overglaze transfers than by lithography. Screen-printing is based on an oriental stencilling method. Colour is forced through a tightly stretched fabric which has some areas blanked out to form a pattern. 'Budding Bough', one of Pountneys', and indeed the industry's, first screen-printed patterns, was designed in 1949.

In their quest for efficiency Pountneys also called in work-study consultants; 'time and motion' was a new fashion in the 1950s. But despite all these innovations, a great deal still needed to be done to the Fishponds factory, by now half a century old. When George Wood was recruited from Stoke-on-Trent in 1959 he was struck by the antediluvian nature of the equipment he was expected to use. 'Victorian' was the adjective most frequently chosen by others to describe their workplace, and some managers, several of whom, after a lifetime serving the firm, were unable to see that they had to spend money if profitability was to be maintained. They happily went on promoting Pountneys as a 'showpiece', even though Wedgwood's new factory at Barlaston, near Stoke-on-Trent, was considerably more advanced.

NOTES

1. Smith and Tyler.
2. Burlington House exhibition, catalogue no.13, dinner set, and Design Council archive photograph, pattern no.2206, 1959.
3. Davis and Dagger.
4. Creed.
5. BMAG X10, 843A.
6. Smith.
7. Duffett.
8. BRO 20165/35.
9. *Pottery and Glass*, October 1948, p. 28.

Bright and modern: pottery 1940–1960

During the Second World War drastic government quotas were imposed on home-market sales whilst exports, particularly to America, were encouraged. Fortunately for Pountneys, they already had a substantial export order-book. From 1941 to 1952, under the Government's 'Utility' scheme, all pottery for the home market had to be undecorated and made in a limited range of shapes. One Bristol design, although not strictly functional, must have met with official approval; their Winston Churchill figures were a popular wartime novelty. Some work remained for the band-and-line shop, however, decorating tableware for hospitals and the forces. Charlie Smith found time to paint a plate with three humorous watchmen. This hung in the showroom, the fire-watch's H.Q.

Patterned crockery could be bought directly from the factory as long as pre-war stocks lasted. When one lady's home was blitzed and all her possessions destroyed, her daughter took her to Pountneys where she particularly admired the 'Olde English' Georgian couple on a dinner-set, saying it reminded her of some embroidered pillow-slips she had owned. To her delight it was later delivered as a surprise gift to her house. The set is now in Bristol Museum and Art Gallery; date-stamps show it was made in 1939.

The Labour Party returned to power in 1945, promising social reform, and education was given priority. The Council of Industrial Design, which became the Design Council, took on the task of improving public taste and commercial design. In 1946 it organised the 'Britain Can Make It' exhibition at the Victoria and Albert Museum. This whetted the appetite for well-designed goods not yet in the shops, and showed overseas buyers that the British were still a match for the world market.

Pountneys figured prominently in the exhibition. Addressing the Design and Industries Association, Alick Newsom said that seven out of their 12 designs submitted had been accepted, in addition to two made by the firm especially for Heals.[1] Three designs by Pountneys' new consultant Agnes Pinder-Davies were shown. Her previous work included interiors for the ships the *Queen Mary*, the *Queen Elizabeth* and the *Mauretania*. The Pottery's decorating manager, Cecil Garland, and his chief paintress, Seraphima Hamblin, were represented, but Charlie Smith's 'Blue Scroll', an adaptation of a traditional motif, was not credited to him. Another painted design, 'Bellflower', had been designed by J. F. Price in 1940.

'Bellflower' is significantly different from Pountneys' products of the 1930s; the glaze is ivory-coloured rather than 'Amberone', and the brush-strokes are crisper and more rhythmic. It foreshadowed a subtle modification of the Bristol hand-painting style which reflected changing fashion. Many designs from this period were by the paintresses, who by now thoroughly understood J. F. Price's interpretation of delftware; Frances Ashman created the sinuous 'Passion Flower', a favourite with American customers[2] and select shops. They sometimes took ideas from other designers; a trial plate painted by Miss Ashman shortly after the war was copied from Swedish tableware illustrated alongside some Bristol Pottery in Gordon Forsyth's *20th Century Ceramics*, published around 1935.[3]

Pountneys continued to work with the Council of Industrial Design in its efforts to raise standards of taste. In June 1949 the Council's travelling 'design fair' stopped for a week at Bristol Museum and Art Gallery. On 14 June the *Bristol Evening Post* illustrated a coffee-set by Cecil Garland with stencilled white birds against a sage-green ground, designed in 1945.[4] This was included in the 1951 Festival of Britain. 'Bellflower' was also exhibited at the Festival. Printing was represented by 'Budding Bough', designed for Pountneys in 1949 by A. Sayer-Smith, with screen-printed transfers made by Johnson Matthey.[5]

The *Evening Post* article referred to the Council's 'considerable amount of education work'; information packs and film strips about design were available for schools, women's organisations and retail shops, 'to enable them to educate their staffs on the subject'. One of the 'Design Folios' dedicated to ceramics highlighted the functional qualities of 12 'good' designs. Plate six showed:

> A hand-painted milk-jug in earthenware made at the Bristol Pottery by Pountney and Company Limited. This simple, barrel-shaped container with its large, beautifully moulded lip and sturdy handle is decorated very appropriately in a cool blue leaf pattern on a dazzling white glaze. The brush-work is vigorous and free, entirely in keeping with the chunky form of the jug...
>
> The 'paintress' – so girls who do this work are called – has used a full brush of colour in the most pleasing and virile manner to produce an effect that is extremely pleasing.[6]

The author was not to know that Charlie Smith was the only person able to execute 'Blue Scroll'. Although strongly influenced by delftware and Torquay pottery, it was very much his own invention. He recalled its conception in the early 1930s:

> Back in years ago they had a rough, rough sort of scroll, and they asked if I'd make it up into a nice, clean pattern, put it that way, see. But at any rate I did it and they were very pleased. And they sent it up to the Chelsea Arts exhibition, for freehand painting, and it won first prize!

I won, but Mr Johnston was in charge of the job, he put his name to it. It became very popular, it did, you know, the world-wide over. The Americans used to think it was wonderful.

'Blue Scroll' was one of Bristol's best-loved patterns. Mr Smith continued to paint it, at home, long after the Pottery closed. It was particularly successful once Utility restrictions were lifted in 1952; after years of plain pottery, retailers and customers must have delighted in its strong colour. Another bright hand-painted pattern, 'Tulip', was also well-received in the 1950s, although a 1928 photograph of the decorating shop showed shelves full of it.

In 1956 the *Bristol Evening Post* described Bristol Corporation's 5,000-piece 'Boston'-shaped dinner-service and two new lines by Pountneys, one emphasising the company's long history, the other looking forward to the future.[7] 'Bristol Scenes' reproduced underglaze transfer-prints based on early 19th century engravings, first used at the Bristol Pottery around 1825. T.B. Johnston could not have foreseen that this type of dense, traditional engraving would return to popularity in the post-war period, along with reproduction antique furniture and 'ye-olde-oak-beamed' interiors. When W.J. Pountney asked after the original copper plates whilst preparing *Old Bristol Potteries*, he found they had just been sold to a scrap merchant.[8] The re-issue, on the fancy-edged 'Gadroon' shape, was made with a new set of copper-plates, painstakingly copied by Reg Hanks from original pieces. In 1959 the firm also re-introduced 'Pheasant', another traditional engraving, last made around 1920.[9]

The second innovation was 'Mooncurve', an ultra-modern shape. In the 1950s the pottery industry was greatly influenced by trends in America, where more casual lifestyles had stimulated a demand for new products. Smaller services, which could be built up gradually, increasingly featured crockery more suited to the television lounge and patio than the dining-room. New shapes like the rimless 'coupe' plate were at first dismissed by English manufacturers; 'where did you put the mustard?' they wondered. However, once introduced they were received with enthusiasm.[10] 'Mooncurve' was right up-to-date with oval, rimless plates and streamlined teapots and tureens. In May 1956 it won a recommendation from the Council of Industrial Design; details on a photograph in the Design Council archive gave its retail price as £9 for a dinner-set, including purchase tax. It was decorated with 'Seedcress', a spiky black abstract floral engraving by Kenneth Clark, Pountneys' new consultant. 'Mooncurve' was also sold with naturalistic transfers and simple, hand-painted patterns like noughts-and-crosses. Sometimes the hollow pieces would be sprayed with a solid colour which complemented printed motifs on the plates and saucers. This form of decoration was highly typical of the late 1950s and early 1960s.

NOTES

1. *Pottery and Glass*, May 1947, p. 25. 'Britain Can Make It' exhibition catalogue, H.M.S.O., 1946, entries 163–186 and 493–4. Pattern numbers: 1004, Hamblin. 1368, Price. 1373 (dinner- and tea-services for Heals), 1509, Garland. 1515, 1519, 1520, Pinder-Davis. 1527, 'Blue Scroll'.
2. Bristol Chamber of Commerce Journal, c. 1950, off-print.
3. Published by *The Studio*, no date.
4. *Bristol Evening Post*, 14 June 1949.
5. Design Council archive photograph information.
6. Council of Industrial Design, *Design folio for use in schools, book F, pottery*, no date.
7. *Bristol Evening Post*, 6 March 1956, p. 8.
8. Pountney, op. cit., p. 119.
9. BMAG NX1188 and Na1329 a–d.
10. Frances Hannah, *Ceramics*, Bell & Hyman, 1986, p. 80.

The Clifford era: 1961–1969 and beyond

By 1960 the three joint managing directors, Alick Newsom, Patrick Johnston and W.G. Cottrell, had served the company for 135 years between them. As they approached retirement they began to consider the future of the firm they had grown up with. Alick Newsom's son Michael worked at the Pottery in the 1950s but had now found his niche as a sales representative. None of the directors' other children were involved in the firm and so, in the absence of an internal candidate, an outsider would have to be found.

Christopher Clifford had been chairman and managing director of Palissy Pottery in Stoke-on-Trent, but moved to Royal Worcester when it bought his firm in 1958. Pountneys' Board had been impressed with Mr Clifford's record at Palissy and so, when managerial disagreements at Royal Worcester led to his resignation, they invited him to become a joint managing director. Although he was 51, with 33 years in the trade, it was nevertheless felt that he could bring new energy and leadership. His son Michael, recently qualified as a ceramic technician, came to Pountneys as a manager at the same time.

Christopher Clifford joined the Board in late 1961. At the same time, W.G. Cottrell stepped down but continued as company secretary. Within 18 months, both Mr Newsom and Mr Johnston had also retired and Mr Clifford became chairman and sole managing director.[1] Another new recruit to the Board was Alan Coghill-Smith, sales director until 1971.

Christopher Clifford was probably well aware that he was taking control of an unprofitable industrial dinosaur. It was still regularly described as 'one of the most modern potteries in the United Kingdom',[2] but, despite its tunnel kilns and the new machinery purchased in the 1950s, the Edwardian 'model' factory was still largely intact. The indigenous Bristol workforce may have been unaware of the extent to which re-tooling had been carried out by rival potteries in Stoke-on-Trent, but they knew all too well that their working conditions had hardly changed since the 1930s.

Indeed the 400-strong workforce itself was getting old. Mr Storey, assistant director and company accountant, drew up a list of 29 'personnel with service of 40 years and upwards',[3] on which his own name ranked fourth. He had started in July 1909, five months after Reg Hanks and three years after Ben Jenkin, the clay foreman. Emily Short, an overglaze decorator, began working for Pountneys in 1903. A long-service award ceremony was held for them in October 1963, and the *Pottery Gazette* reported that Miss Short, like most of the other recipients, wanted to work as long as possible.[4] On the whole the elderly workers were still needed; although Pountneys paid slightly higher wages than Stoke-on-Trent firms, pottery manufacture was one of the lowest-paid industries. Jobs in Bristol's engineering, packaging, confectionery and tobacco industries were more lucrative and Pountneys found recruitment increasingly difficult.

Christopher Clifford made sweeping changes in an effort to bring the Pottery up-to-date. Work spaces were rearranged to improve efficiency; the overglaze-decorating department's benches were replaced by a production line system which, it was claimed, 'avoids unnecessary movements and considerably reduces human handling with its attendant breakage hazards'.[5] Processes were speeded up; the number of trucks going through the enamel kilns was increased from 16 to 24 each day. Even the packing department was transformed; in 1965 the firm announced that:

> Non-returnable cartons in two sizes . . . are to be used for packaging, with prices quoted inclusive right through to the shop. Each item is to be placed first in polythene, to keep it 'clean and factory fresh', as Mr Clifford remarked.[6]

Every activity was assessed for profitability; in 1965 considerable savings were made when the entire sales staff was dismissed and that side of the business was contracted-out.

The product itself was reviewed. The most important change came in October 1962 when the name, goodwill, moulds and pattern books of Royal Cauldon were acquired.[7] This well-known Stoke-on-Trent company, established in 1792, had gone into liquidation and Pountneys seized the opportunity to purchase several successful, Victorian-looking designs. At the same time, work began on a new shape to replace 'Mooncurve'. 'Clifton', launched in 1965, had standard, interchangeable parts, and was mainly decorated with comparatively cheap overglaze-printed patterns. 'Bristol Garden', produced shortly afterwards, involved no decorating, since it was plain white. A profitable trade in litho-printed advertising and souvenir goods was also developed from the mid-1960s whilst sanitary castings and hotel ware became less important.

None of these efforts brought about an economic miracle. The huge factory was too old and inflexible to survive in an increasingly competitive industry. Most successful potteries were well-equipped with the latest technology and managerial expertise. Many family firms were going out of business; between 1956 and 1963 the number of tableware manufacturers in Britain dropped from 130 to 94.[8] Since then the industry has been transformed by a series of mergers, closures and buy-outs.

In 1968, in order to repay debts totalling £110,000, the Board agreed to sell the factory site, its most important asset. Generous grants were available to firms relocating in Industrial Development Areas and so it was decided to move the whole concern to a trading estate at Pool, between Camborne and Redruth in Cornwall. There, labour was plentiful and wages were low.

The Fishponds site was put on the market in the summer of 1968 and on 17 September Mr Clifford accepted an offer of £235,000 from MacKenzie Hill Investments Limited of London. The relocation scheme began immediately. Staff and operatives were told that in 12 months the factory would close.

There had been some suspicion that all was not well, but nevertheless this came as a great shock. The blow was not softened by the assurance that some men, chosen from volunteers, could be taken on at Camborne. Although over half the workforce were women, they were not encouraged to move; it was supposed that they had family commitments in Bristol. Exploratory coach-trips left most of the workers and their wives un-impressed. The little industrial town was far from being the type of picturesque Cornish village with which they were familiar. Four hours from Bristol by train and taking the full blast of the Atlantic's winter winds, it seemed like 'the back of beyond' to Charles Harman. Les Cockram said he had 'never been so cold in all his life'. The council houses he looked at were small, rents were high and the nearest school was five miles away. Most workers, like Mr Harman, never considered moving because their families were firmly rooted in Bristol:

> At that time the eldest girl was 15 or 16. Her exam period was coming up. I said, 'There's no way I'm going to move those children from their schools. . .' We'd bought this tiny little terraced house. . . I could see the factory from the back of the garden. . . With shift work it had taken us umpteen years to get it right. . . I'd paid it off in ten years so it was off our backs, so I said 'Forget it'.

The management must have been dismayed when, instead of a queue of eager volunteers, only a handful of skilled potters were prepared to move, and several of those for just a few months.

Despite the financial difficulties, Bristol's order books were still full, but as they went about their work, 'a lot of people had this on their minds for all those weeks'.[9] The Union's membership records tell their own story as the workforce dwindled and surnames familiar for generations at the Pottery ceased to appear in the registers.[10]

> I think people were acting a bit brave, saying 'Oh, I can get a job here,' but then it was the first million out of work at that time, and a lot of us didn't realise how old we was. I didn't realise I was 40 until I went down the training centre to see if I could get a job, and I thought, 'All

of a sudden I'm old!' – a couple of places said 'Oh, we want someone about 35'.[11]

Autumn 1969 came at last. Redundancy notices were given to the remaining workers, and payments of between £300 and £900. Each received a brief testimonial and they gathered with the management for farewell handshakes. Phyllis Creed remembered leaving at dinner-time on her last day: Friday 10 October. The factory seemed deserted as she walked the route she had taken every week for 40 years:

> Everybody else had gone. We had to go through the dipping house, round by the kilns and out through the saggars shop and all the way round. I went all out by myself. Oh, I did feel dejected and sad.

She recorded that day in her diary:

> I finished work at Pountneys today. I did 5 bowls in gold. Awful saying Goodbye to everyone. I cried all the way home, but enjoyed dinner. Didn't feel like going out so after a little doze we played Scrabble until tea.[12]

Miss Creed was offered a job in a doll factory, but nursed her sick mother instead. Some workers found employment in the engineering industry, but many discovered their expertise was of little use and they had to take less skilled work. Those nearing retirement were among the worst hit since, by being made redundant, they lost their rights to the small company pension. Few found their new workplaces as enjoyable as Pountneys used to be, or the work as satisfying.

All the Pottery's unwanted plant and machinery was auctioned on 18 December 1969. The building was demolished and the site is now an industrial estate.

The move to Cornwall; Cauldon Bristol Potteries Limited

It was important for the Bristol Pottery, which intended to continue trading and expand in its new home, to present the move in a positive light. The closure was first reported by the *Bristol Evening Post* on 12 November 1968:

> Mr Clifford said the Fishponds factory was too large due to modern methods needing less floor space. Also it was difficult to get all the labour they wanted... The move was to a development area to which the Government was trying to attract industry. This would bring the firm grants to make it financially worth while... Also labour was available, and the raw material was mined locally.
>
> 'We are very busy and the export trade is flourishing, but under the present conditions we are having great difficulty in executing our orders quickly enough,' said Mr Clifford.

The following day another article appeared under the headline 'POTTERY'S MOVE WILL NOT CAUSE HARDSHIP' in which Mr Clifford assured the paper that:

> Because of the prosperity of this city and the low level of unemployment, it is not thought there will be any difficulty in them finding jobs. . . The Potters' Union are concerned that any should have to be made redundant, but they are content with the company's plans for redundancy payment and assisting with finding work.

Excited optimism pervaded subsequent press articles as details of the new factory were revealed. On 4 January 1969 the *New Observer* announced that work had started on the £200,000 building, but by February progress was halted by blizzards. Its vast ready-made tunnel kilns were delivered by a three-day journey the following June and by late July, Cornish trainees were making their first pottery,[13] supervised by around 18 key-workers from Bristol and others from Stoke-on-Trent. On 1 November 1969 the new factory officially opened, Pountneys changed its name to Cauldon Bristol Potteries Limited, and a new era began.

The backstamp 'Royal Cauldon Bristol Ironstone' had been used since 1967 on pottery derived from Royal Cauldon patterns, notably the 'Bristol Garden' range of moulded white tableware, and this was now adopted for all the firm's products. ('Ironstone' was included for the benefit of American customers who tended to be disdainful of earthenware.) 'Bristol Garden', and Cauldon's 'Victoria' and 'Bittersweet' patterns were to be the leading lines and so the change of name was an obvious choice. The emphasis was now very much on export markets, particularly North and South America. In March 1969 the *Illustrated Bristol News* had commented that Mr Clifford and Mr Coghill-Smith were 'both hard sellers, pounding the export beats every year and every year increasing the size of the order book.'[14] Advertising ceramics would still be made alongside tableware, but the manufacture of hotel crockery and sanitary castings ceased.

The building was only half finished when the first firing took place in July 1969, but the new Cornish workers made a happy team. About 160 local people were eventually employed. *Tableware International* reported that, 'The staff recruited in this area have a very definite sympathy with pottery production not always found in other parts of the country'.[15] The majority were women, used to seasonal hotel work, but willing to learn and to take on a variety of jobs. Audrey Coleman, born and bred in Cornwall, came to the Pottery from a laundry. She enjoyed fettling and sponging the most. Salt and pepper pots were her favourites, 'because there wasn't much to do. And on the top there were six or seven holes for the pepper and one for the salt. You'd got to look at all the tops and then if one was faulty you'd put it right.'

Christopher Clifford shared T.B. Johnston's ambition to build and design a completely new pottery, but whilst Johnston's factory was a lasting achievement, the move to Cornwall failed. Six months later the Pottery's order books were worryingly empty, and within two years it was bankrupt.

Many factors contributed to the collapse, including commercial mis-judgement and underestimation of the difficulty of making quality ware with such an inexperienced workforce. It was also hard to operate effectively in such an isolated location. 'The clean air of Camborne...a very short haul from clay, the white harvest of St. Austell'[16] may have seemed attractive, but the raw materials actually came all the way from Stoke-on-Trent.

External factors played a part, for instance the onset of the deep recession which blighted world trade in the 1970s. The pottery industry was particularly hit by President Nixon's introduction of import tariffs. In Britain, the pub ashtray business suffered when increased taxes on cigarettes and tobacco led to cuts in advertising budgets.

In September 1971 an article in *Tableware International* entitled 'Cornish move gives Cauldon Bristol an exciting future' echoed uncannily a description of the Fishponds factory which appeared in the *Pottery Gazette* in 1905,[17] but on 26 November Bristolians must have read with amazement the *Evening Post's* announcement of the firm's liquidation. The final blow had come when:

> Only this week, the company had been successful in tendering for a £100,000 contract to supply coffee mugs to a petroleum company... 'We geared up our production to meet this contract, only to discover on Wednesday that the oil company had changed their mind and were giving away plastic mugs instead,' Mr Clifford told employees... yesterday, in the face of an empty order book, Mr William Eggins, a receiver and manager appointed by Cauldon's bankers, moved into the factory with the task of salvaging the remaining assets and searching for a buyer.

In December 1971 Cauldon Bristol was purchased by A.G. Richardson & Co. Limited, the Stoke-on-Trent manufacturers of Crown Ducal Ware. Their rescue attempts included selling Pountneys' valuable delftware collection, inviting the chairman of Redruth and Camborne Urban District Council to officially 'open' the factory in May 1972, launching 'Polly', 'a brown tea set with old-world overtones', commissioned by Habitat, and relaunching a transfer-print version of 'Blue Scroll'.[18]

The name Royal Cauldon was adopted by Crown Ducal. In the early 1970s they bought Browns of Ferrybridge in Yorkshire and, when the Cornish factory closed in 1977, it was re-named Cauldon Potteries.

Browns had been founded in 1793, just a year later than Royal Cauldon. Since 1983 Cauldon Potteries Limited (Ferrybridge) has been part of the Perks Ceramics Group.

NOTES

1. *Pottery and Glass*, February 1962, p. 302, and July 1963, p. 769.
2. *Pottery and Glass*, July 1963, p. 769.
3. Company record, copy in BMAG.
4. *Pottery Gazette*, October 1963, p. 1097.
5. *Pottery Gazette*, January 1962, p. 112.
6. *Pottery and Glass*, April 1965, p. 448.
7. *Pottery Gazette*, November 1962, p. 1291.
8. Frances Hannah, *Ceramics*, Bell & Hyman, 1986, p. 86.
9. Wood.
10. Ceramic and Allied Trades Union archive, Stoke-on-Trent.
11. Wood.
12. Private collection, copy in BMAG.
13. *Bristol Evening Post*, 22 February, 20 June, and 22 July, 1969.
14. *Illustrated Bristol News*, March 1969.
15. *Tableware International*, September 1971, p. 80.
16. *Illustrated Bristol News*, loc. cit.
17. *Tableware International*, September 1971, p. 78. *Pottery Gazette*, September 1905, p. 1006.
18. *Tableware International*, May 1972, p. 64.

'Mooncurve' shape, probably designed by Kenneth Clark, 1955–65. Left to right: Tureen and cover with sprayed body and 'Meadow Vetch' overglaze-print. *Na1107*. Sales card for 'Golden Days', *Central Library*, *B22719*. Coffee-pot and cover, underglaze-painted hotel-ware pattern with underglaze-printed badge 'THE COMMODORE', *Na1060*. Plate, 'Seedcress' underglaze-print, designed by Kenneth Clark. Teapot, sprayed body and 'Harvest Home' overglaze-print, *Na1323*. Plate, underglaze-painted, *Na514*.

'Boston' shape: Part-coffee-service and breakfast cup, with overglaze banding-and-lining and screen-printed 'Budding Bough' pattern designed by A. Sayer-Smith for Johnson Matthey transfers, 1949. Exhibited at the 'Festival of Britain', 1951.

Right, Reg Hanks designing a 'badge' for hotel-ware. 1959. *X10, 710A.*
Bottom, 'Mooncurve' shape with sprayed borders and overglaze-printing: Cup and saucer, coffee-pot and jug, 'Lilybell', 1961. Left plate, 'Longleat', right plate, 'Badminton', both 1962. Sales brochures for 'Cotswold' and 'Lilybell', *Central Library B22719.*

89

Bristol Scenes

These reproductions of 18th century West Country scenes after designs by Nicholas Pocock, depict amongst others, the Avon Gorge, Hotwells, St. Vincents Rocks, Chepstow and Monmouth. Full Dinner and Tea Services are available in semi-Porcelain on the distinct Gadroon shape in Royal Blue and Ripe Strawberry.

An illustrated brochure will be gladly sent on request.

Lovely 18th Century scenes of Old Bristol

EACH PIECE CARRYING ON THE REVERSE THIS IDENTIFICATION

Reproduced by Craftsmen at

THE BRISTOL POTTERY

Advertisement for 'Bristol Scenes', underglaze-printed on 'Gadroon' shape. *Pottery Gazette*, November 1956, p. 1527.

Cecil Garland's retirement presentation, August 1962. *Pottery Gazette*, September 1962, p. 1103. Cecil Garland N.R.D. became assistant decorating manager in 1933, and manager in the post-war years. Patrick Johnston shakes his hand and Christopher Clifford looks on. Charles Harman, then in charge of the enamel kiln, is on the left at the back, next to Bert Duffett, with glasses, and Charlie Smith. *X10, 479A*.

Glost sorters with the last sanitary castings fired at Bristol, 1969. Left-hand group, Mrs Abraham, Bert Duffett, Barbara Heap. Kneeling on right, Les Cockram, glost sorting manager. *X10, 640A*.

'Clifton' shape with overglaze-printed 'Kudu' pattern, designed by Pat Chewter, 1965.

'Longline' kitchen-ware range, with underglaze-prints designed by Honor Elliot, 1961. Measuring-jug shape designed by J.F. Price, 1934. Large shaker, *Na1126*. Rolling-pin, *Na1125*. Cruet, marked; 'AWARDED THE OFFICIAL SEAL OF THE GOOD HOUSEKEEPING INSTITUTE', *Na513*. Brochure, Central Library, B227719.

The last years: pottery from the 1960s

In October 1961, 'Lilybell', an overglaze floral print, was launched on the 'Mooncurve' shape. An advertisement in the *Illustrated Bristol News* described it:

> This design has that unmistakable air that three centuries of good breeding bestows. Charmingly sophisticated, elegant in line and design, Lilybell is a study in silver-grey; the silver edge band is in perfect harmony with the subtle shades of the delicate flower motif. A true Bristol beauty.[1]

'Lilybell' and 'Cotswold', with wild flowers in an olive border, were created by the Pottery's design team, now headed by Kenneth Clark, a well-known freelance consultant. Customers liked their classic prettiness and so 'Badminton' and 'Longleat' continued the theme in spring 1962.[2]

It might be supposed that these rather safe designs reflected the tastes of a Board of Directors approaching retirement. However, another new range demonstrated their willingness to please younger customers. Bristol's 'Long Line' kitchen-ware, decorated with bold underglaze-printed cutlery, was featured in the *Woman's Journal* 'House of the Year 1962' at Coombe Dingle, Bristol, and won a recommendation from the Good Housekeeping Institute.[3] It was created by Honor Elliot, at 23, the youngest member of the design team. She came to Bristol in 1959 fresh from college in Stoke-on-Trent. Her father had a cutlery business in Sheffield, which perhaps explains the motif, but it was generally popular at the time. Some shapes went back to J.F. Price's kitchen-ware line developed in the 1930s, but they still managed to look contemporary alongside streamlined 1960s coffee-pots and cruets.

In 1963 Honor Elliot also designed a range of kitchen and tableware; this featured oven-to-table pieces, a new concept which reflected changing eating habits. Its decoration, however, was an adaptation of a cheerful pattern on an 18th century delftware dish in the company's museum. This overglaze print, 'applied by a method of reproducing hand brush strokes by mechanical means', was, at first sight, a very convincing imitation of hand-painting.[4]

Pountneys' appreciation of youthful talent reflected a trend in the industry; in 1958 Royal College of Art students had created W.T. Copelands' popular 'Apollo' range. An emphasis on youth became apparent in society as a whole as the teenagers of the 1950s became significant consumers in the 1960s. However, traditional designs continued to have a wide appeal; indeed the Victorian theme, which was to be of such commercial importance, emerged in the 'pop-art' years.

Christopher Clifford's first major step at Pountneys was to purchase Royal Cauldon in October 1962. *Pottery and Glass* commented:

> Retail distributors of high quality domestic earthenware will welcome the news. . .that the fine old name Cauldon is to continue. Its acquisition by Britain's oldest established pottery manufacturer. . . suggests that this famous name is in very safe and sound keeping. The 'Royal Victoria' pattern, regarded by some as having been in the 'Top Ten' for several decades, and stocked for generations by a very large number of distributors, will continue to be available. . .
>
> 'Royal Victoria' is of early 19th century design, and was bought by Queen Victoria for use in the Royal Household. On the shape 'Wessex', which has a scalloped edge, the decoration consists of a multi-coloured, border-width litho, with spray inside the cup, hand-painted handles and knobs, and gold edge finish.[5]

Although the Royal Cauldon backstamp was still used, all Cauldon pieces made between 1963 and 1969 came from Fishponds. 'Bittersweet', another early Victorian Cauldon pattern, originally made by Coalport or Coalbrookdale, was an underglaze all-over floral print with hand-coloured details. Cauldon products were quite different from Pountneys' usual output. The paintresses found 'Bittersweet' 'much more interesting work'[6] than the simple dashes and squiggles of the 'Mooncurve' era, although it was less challenging than the complicated freehand patterns they used to do. Unlike the hand-painting on which Bristol's reputation had been built, these good quality, traditional prints did not depend on the artistry of a few experienced individuals, but could be reproduced by anyone with the right training. Pountneys' acquisition of 'Victoria' in 1962 was probably based on some market research; Royal Albert's famous 'Old Country Roses', in the same vein as 'Victoria', was first made in that year.

A new modern shape was urgently needed, in addition to 'Victoria's' classic 'Wessex' shape. Pat Chewter, lecturer in charge of ceramics at Liverpool College of Art, succeeded Kenneth Clark as Pountneys' consultant designer, and remained with the firm until 1971. In 1965 he developed 'Clifton', which was greeted enthusiastically by the *Pottery Gazette*:

> Sharp curves have been eliminated from the contours, giving teapots and cups an angular handle which is large and easy to hold. Three different cup shapes share the same size handle (there is a coffee beaker, a tall cup and a shallow one particularly for overseas); the saucer also fits each. As well as a covered scollop, there is a three-pint round casserole with convenient flanges matching those of the cream soup. The soup stand also serves as a base for the sauce boat, and coupe plates go with the modern decorations while traditional rimmed flat [plates] match the more classical style. A distinctive oval meat dish

94

with an angled rim provided difficulties of potting which seemed insuperable at first, but which were finally overcome with satisfaction. With a new shape, much of the responsibility falls on the modeller, and Mr George Wood at Bristol did sterling work.[7]

The need to rationalise shapes so that a set needed a minimum number of different parts was an important consideration with labour becoming increasingly scarce. The article then described 'Clifton's' litho decorations:

Perhaps the most characteristic of Bristol Pottery is one which Mr Chewter has adopted from patterns traditional to the factory such as 'Blue Scroll'... Called 'Medici', the twentieth century version is a clean repeat motif in Oxford and Cambridge blues. Perhaps the most striking, and likely to have immediate impact on the young moderns, is 'Sunset Boulevard', a series of abstract motifs in brilliant red on a background of two different green shades. There is, too, 'Sherwood' textile-inspired in line with today's taste, and based on ragged patterns of green and black. 'Kudu', in blue, black and brown, gives a surrealist impression of the African antelope from which its name is devised [sic] – a mobile and interesting pattern.

'Clifton' was sometimes hand-painted; 'Blue Scroll' itself looked well on it, and Charlie Smith used to devote Saturday mornings to fulfilling all the American orders. It was decided to produce a litho-transfer from his hand-work to meet the demand and to ensure its continuation:

They did a transfer, but all the hollow-ware they couldn't transfer very well – they couldn't get the cups in sequence so that they all joined up together. So I did the pieces they couldn't do, I painted them, and they put it over to the American market as hand-painted. They had it all sent back![8]

A new clay recipe was developed at the same time. 'Bristol White' was a blue-white, in contrast to the creamy-whites which had dominated the trade for years. In the age of 'Bri-nylon', and soap powders with optical brighteners to make them 'wash whiter', the old crockery seemed dull and retailers clamoured for a 'pure' white body.

'Clifton' also launched a new backstamp featuring the *Matthew*, in which John Cabot sailed from Bristol to discover Newfoundland in 1497. Since this was only used until 1969, it is almost as rare as examples of 'Clifton' itself. The shape was intended to revive the Pottery's flagging fortunes, but sales were poor. Quick action was called for, and so Alan Coghill-Smith, the sales director, undertook to develop a new line with Pat Chewter. He liked the Victorian 'look' and so, because all Pountneys' 19th century moulds had been thrown away, he searched through the old Cauldon moulds that had come to Bristol in 1962. He eventually came across some Victorian plates with embossed trellis-and-flower borders. They were intended for bone china, not earthenware, and only about a third of the shapes needed were there, so George Wood began the fiddly task of modelling an entire range, with shapes to suit both domestic and overseas markets.

'Bristol Garden', launched in February 1967, was the result, and its combination of Victorian charm with 'sixties' styling was a runaway success. It heralded a generation of plain white moulded designs, and anticipated the romantic Victorian look of the 1970s and 1980s. On the advice of Susie Cooper, Pountneys later developed variants, with the flowers picked out in overglaze-prints, called 'June Garden', 'Autumn Garden' and 'Winter Garden'.

Like 'Victoria', 'Bristol Garden' made a striking contrast to Pountneys' delftware-inspired *repertoire*. The Bristol style's day was probably over, even if the Pottery had not closed; it was too bold and colourful for 1970s taste. Moreover, few British potteries could maintain skilled hand-painters, and the problems of the 'Blue Scroll' transfer-print illustrate the difficulty of reproducing painting in print in those days.

Only one more major shape was developed at Bristol, a plainer style than 'Bristol Garden', with moulded beadings. The Cornish factory relied on orders for these two, the perennial 'Victoria' and sets of fancy plates aimed at the emergent collectors' market, which was particularly strong in America. Based on moulded Cauldon originals, these were decorated with four series of transfers: 'Caribbean Flowers', 'Wild Flowers', 'American Birds' and 'French Fruits'.

The beaded shape was decorated with printed *chinoiserie* and delftware designs. Its last pattern, 'Cluny', based on a medieval tile, was launched by A.G. Richardson in September 1972.[9] One Bristol creditor had been paid in lorry loads of 'Bristol Garden', and the last remains of this consignment were sold by Fletchers of Stapleton Road in 1990. Apart from this, the piles of unused 'Cluny' transfers, in the stores at Cauldon Potteries, are almost the only reminders of the Bristol Pottery's last days in Cornwall.

One or two moulds for embossed plates are also preserved at Ferrybridge, but most of Pountneys' and Royal Cauldons' moulds were destroyed in the early 1980s. As for the other items which, together with moulds and transfer sheets, represent the 'life-blood' of a pottery, apart from a few chance survivals, the company's vast stocks of engraved copper-plates were scrapped in 1969. Volume upon volume of pattern books, starting in the last century and ending with Cecil Garland's meticulous illustrations, were made into a bonfire.

NOTES

1. *Illustrated Bristol News*, October 1961, advertisement section.
2. *Pottery and Glass*, February 1962, p. 287, April 1962, p. 320.
3. *Pottery and Glass*, April 1962, and backstamp.
4. *Pottery and Glass*, September 1963, p. 991. Charger illustrated in *Pottery and Glass*, July 1952, p. 53.
5. *Pottery and Glass*, November 1962, p. 1291 and p. 1310.
6. Creed.
7. *Pottery Gazette*, April 1965, p. 446.
8. Smith.
9. *Tableware International*, September 1972, p. 81.

Appendix: Backstamps used by the Bristol Pottery

At least 40 different backstamps were used by *Pountneys* between 1905 and 1969, but they fall into distinct categories datable to within a few years. A representative selection are shown below. In addition, impressed date stamps giving the month and year of manufacture are usually found on plates and meat dishes, whilst this information was often scratched on hollow-ware. Date stamping was discontinued around 1960. Other marks include painted four-figure pattern numbers and paintresses' or litho-transferers' identification numbers or letters.

1. 'Established 1750': pre-c.1923.

This was used until the publication of W.J. Pountney's book *Old Bristol Potteries* in 1920, which showed that the Temple Back Pottery's deeds went back to 1683.

2. Tradenames: pre-c.1925

POUNTNEYS
BRISTOL SEMI CHINA
SUTHERLAND PATTERN

3. 'Established 1683': c.1922–c.1948.

Bristol
WARE
POUNTNEY & Cº Lᵀᴰ
BRISTOL.
ENGLAND.
ESTᴰ 1683.

Bristol
Est. 1683
Pountney & Co.Ltd
Made in England

4. Art wares and artists' private work.

The Bristol
'Fiscal' Pottery

Decoration by
The Bristol
Porcelain
Painters
1750 ——— 19
The Bristol
Pottery   Eng.

POUNTNEY'S
BRISTOL
"COCK & HEN"
POTTERY.

C.J. GARLAND NRD
BRISTOL

BRISTOL
HAND PAINTED
CAS

5. 'Modern Bristol': c.1934–c.1940.
This was used on the shapes designed by J.F. Price, and includes their names, such as 'Dorland', 'Academy' and 'Burlington'. However, these shapes sometimes have other backstamps.

MODERN ═══
BRISTOL ═══
DORLAND
SHAPE
REGISTERED Nº 789752
IN UNITED KINGDOM
POUNTNEY&Cº Lᵀᴰ
"NEWLYN"
——— MADE IN
═══ GREAT BRITAIN

99

6. 'Vitrite': c.1909–1969.

Vitrite was Pountneys' toughened ceramic body, used for hotel wares.

7. 'Founded in 1652': c.1945–1957 (with crossed swords)
1957–1965 (without crossed swords)

A delftware fragment bearing the date 1652, now in Bristol Museum and
Art Gallery, had been excavated in 1914 by W.J. Pountney at the site of the
Brislington Pottery. The Bristol Pottery began to use this date in the late
1940s.

   Crossed swords, in imitation of the famous Meissen porcelain mark,
have been used by many potteries, including Richard Champion's factory
which made hard-paste porcelain in Bristol 1770–1781. Pountneys used
them on various backstamps from the Victorian period onwards.

8. 'Established 1652', with ship: 1965–1969.

This backstamp features the *Matthew*, the ship in which John Cabot
sailed from Bristol to discover Newfoundland in 1497.

Made in England

9.   Royal Cauldon: 1963–1969.

Royal Cauldon was acquired by the Bristol Pottery late in 1962 and the Cauldon backstamp was used from then onwards at the Fishponds factory.

10.   'Royal Cauldon Bristol Ironstone' 1967–1972.

This was used mainly on pottery derived from Royal Cauldon patterns made at Bristol from 1967, and exclusively at the Cornwall factory from July 1969. Apart from hand-painting and underglaze-printing the same products were made at both factories.

11. 'Reproduction delftware' and '1770–1781' marks.

A variety of these were used throughout the factory's history on patterns inspired by tin-glazed earthenware, which was made in the Bristol area in the 17th and 18th centuries, and Bristol hard-paste porcelain, made by Richard Champion at Bristol 1770–1781.

Old Bristol
18ᵗʰ Century
POUNTNEY & CO LTD
BRISTOL
ENGLAND
ESTᵈ 1683

REPRODUCTION OF
Bristol
founded 1652
England
OLD BRISTOL DELFT

Bristol
1770 X 1781
Reproduced
by
Pountney & Co
England

OLD BRISTOL DELFT
A D 1652 ·1780
A reproduction of the famous
hand-painted Tulip Pattern
made at the Bristol Pottery. circa 1680

THE BRISTOL POTTERY
BRISTOL . ENGLAND
FOUNDED 1652

12. Kitchen-ware.

BRISTOL
"LONG LINE"
KITCHEN WARE

BY
POUNTNEY & CO. LTD.
THE BRISTOL POTTERY
BRISTOL
ENGLAND

AWARDED THE OFFICIAL SEAL
OF THE
GOOD HOUSEKEEPING INSTITUTE

Further Reading

Major works and other publications not referred to in the footnotes

ANON. *Ceramics in Bristol: The Fine Wares,* exhibition catalogue, City of Bristol Museum and Art Gallery, 1979.

BURCHILL, Frank, and ROSS, Richard, *A History of the Potters' Union,* Ceramic and Allied Trades Union, Stoke-on-Trent, 1977.

HANNAH, Frances, *Twentieth Century Design: Ceramics,* Bell & Hyman, 1986.

NIBLETT, Kathy, *Dynamic Design; the British Pottery Industry, 1940–1990,* Stoke-on-Trent City Museum and Art Gallery, 1990.

POUNTNEY, W.J. *Old Bristol Potteries,* J.W. Arrowsmith Ltd., Bristol, 1920, reprinted by EP Publishing Ltd., East Ardsley, Yorkshire, 1972.

SARSBY, Jacqueline, *Missuses & Mouldrunners: An oral history of women pottery workers at work and at home*. Open University Press, Milton Keynes, 1988.

Bristol Evening Post:
'Bristol's Oldest Craft', 6 May, 1939, p. 8.
'Focus on Industry: Bristol Pottery', 6 February, 1954, p. 7.

Illustrated Bristol News:
'The Bristol Pottery, Pountney & Co. Ltd.', October 1961, p. 36.
'A New Industry for Cornwall – Bristol's Export', March 1969.

Pottery Gazette:
'The Fiscal Question; Mr T.B. Johnston's views', June 1905, p. 657.
'A New Bristol Pottery', September 1905, p. 1006.
'Buyers' News', June 1909, p. 679.
'Bristol Pottery Old and New', November 1911, p. 1326.
'Welfare Work at the Bristol Pottery', October 1920, p. 1351.
'British Art in Industry Exhibition', February 1935, p. 213.
'The Bristol Story', October 1953, p. 1484.
'Bristol Pottery – New Outlook', April 1965, p. 446.

Pottery and Glass:
'At the Source', July 1945, off-print.
'Bristol Pottery Yesterday and Today', May 1947, p. 24.
'Development', October 1948, p. 28.
'The Bristol Pottery', July 1952, p. 52.
'The Changing face of Bristol Pottery', April 1962, p. 320.

Tableware International:
'Cornish Move Gives Cauldon Bristol an Exciting Future', September 1971, p. 78.
'Cauldon Bristol re-emergent', May 1972, p. 62.